SIMPLY JESUS

SIMPLY JESUS

HIS LIFE AND TEACHINGS IN HISTORICAL ORDER

Notes and Commentary by Jonathan Ziman

Foreword by Dr. Woodrow Kroll

BakerBooks

a division of Baker Publishing Group
Grand Rapids, Michigan

Published by Baker Books
A division of Baker Publishing Group
P.O. Box 6287, Grand Rapids, MI, 49516-6287
www.bakerbooks.com

Previously published under the title *The Life of Jesus*
ISBN 978-0-8010-7247-5

Printed in the United States of America

A portion of the purchase price of this book has been provided to God's Word to the Nations. This mission society is being used by the Holy Spirit to promote and support a movement among God's people to be active participants in his mission "to seek and save people who are lost" (Luke 19:10).

Produced with the assistance of The Livingstone Corporation (www.LivingstoneCorp.com). Project staff includes Betsy Schmitt, Linda Taylor, Ryan Taylor, and Andy Culbertson. Cover design by Larry Taylor. Interior design by Mark Wainwright. Production by Joel Barlett.

12   13   14   15   16   17   18   7   6   5   4   3   2

TABLE OF CONTENTS

FOREWORD

Remember those family vacations with your parents? You probably planned them for your kids too. Everybody had fun. Everybody learned things about geography, the weather, the rest of the family, and themselves.

But if your family is anything like mine, there was one person who saw the family vacation as more than an adventure. One person kept a journal listing everything you did, everything you saw, every place you ate, every unique character you met, and every challenge you had to overcome. Important at the time, their journal is now priceless because it is a written record of what your minds, now far removed from the events, sometimes have trouble remembering.

The Gospel writers were like your family journalist. Wherever Jesus went, whomever He met, whatever challenges He faced, they were there. They kept a record of every important detail. Thanks to Matthew, Mark, Luke, and John, we have accurate, historical, and personal insight into the life of Jesus.

The reason that's important is because Jesus is unlike any other person who ever walked this planet. Jesus is the most unique person ever to live. Think about it.

JESUS' BIRTH WAS UNIQUE

Jesus experienced the most unique birth of anyone who ever lived. His birth was prophesied. He was to be born of a virgin (Isa. 7:14). The town of His birth would be Bethlehem of Judah (Mic. 5:2). He would be born of David's seed (Jer. 33:15–16; Zech. 6:12–13; see Matt. 2:1–2; Luke 1:32–33). Old Testament prophets gave us insight into the life and work of Jesus even before He was born.

But what really makes Jesus' birth unique is not that He was born of a virgin or that His birth took place in a Bethlehem stable, as important as those are. What really makes His birth unique is that Jesus is the only person ever born who is both God and man. Not half-God and half-man. That only makes Him half-human and half-divine. Not even 100 percent God and 100 percent man. That makes Him 200 percent. Jesus is the one-of-a-kind, unique God-man, God in the flesh, Immanuel, God with us. There is simply no one to compare to Him. He is unique.

JESUS' DEATH WAS UNIQUE

What makes Jesus' death so unique? Was it that He was crucified? Was it because He was innocent? Was it because He was a martyr? None of the above. Each of these is an important element in Jesus' death, but it's not what makes His death unique.

Jesus was crucified on a Roman cross, by Roman soldiers, at the insistence of the Jewish religious leaders. But Jesus was not the only person ever to be crucified. In fact, crucifixion was the common Roman form of death in the first century. Nor was Jesus' death unique because He was a martyr. In fact, Jesus was not martyred. The Bible clearly says that He laid down His life for us (1 John 3:16). He died to pay a debt He did not owe, because we owed a debt we could not pay. He paid the penalty for our sins with His life, and that's what makes Jesus' death unique. "God had Christ, who was sinless, take our sin so that we might receive God's approval through him" (2 Cor. 5:21). Jesus died to pay the penalty for your sin and my sin, and no one else ever did, or could.

JESUS' RESURRECTION WAS UNIQUE

That Jesus rose from the grave on the third day after He was crucified is one of the best-attested facts of history. Literally hundreds of people saw Him alive after He had been dead. But what about His resurrection was so unique?

Let's face it. Resurrection is unusual. How many of your deceased friends have you had a latte with recently? The general principle of life, according to the Scriptures, is that "People die once, and after that they are judged" (Heb. 9:27). Resurrection is promised to all in the future, but resurrection shortly after death is the exception to the rule. So what was so unique about Jesus' resurrection? All the other resurrections recorded in the Bible took people by surprise. None were expected, especially by the person who died. But Jesus often spoke about the fact that He would be mocked, scourged, and crucified, but He would rise again on the third day (see Matt. 17:23; 20:19; 26:61; 27:40). Jesus' resurrection was both planned by the Trinity and announced to the laity.

Also, all the other people who were raised from the dead eventually died again and were not resurrected a second time. In other words, their resurrections were unusual, but they were not repeated. When they died a second time they remained dead.

Jesus talked, walked, breathed, and ate with His followers for forty days after that first Resurrection Sunday morning to prove convincingly that He was alive. He then ascended into heaven from the midst of the crowd (Acts 1:9–11) to live eternally, exalted forever at the Father's right hand. No one else can claim such complete victory over death.

JESUS' PERSON WAS UNIQUE

Think of all the interesting people you have met over the years. Some may have been from your hometown, others from that family vacation you took. What makes them so interesting? Is it some unusual gift they have, something special they could do? Is it the way you bonded with them once you got to know them? Maybe it's what they did for you that no one else ever did.

Whatever it is, spend a moment of reflection here to consider just how unique Jesus is in what He did for you.

Jesus changed the life and destiny of every person He encountered who saw in Him the uniqueness of God's Son, our Savior. Why is that? What is there about this Jesus that changes people's lives, both in Bible times and today? Here's what's different about Jesus: He is the only Savior this world will ever have.

Jesus is unique because He is the only person both capable and willing to pay the penalty for *our* sins by dying for *us*, in *our* place, on the cross. Jesus is unique because He can redeem us with His own blood. The Buddhist Catechism says that no one can be redeemed by another. No god and no saint is able to shield a man from the consequences of his evil doings. Every one of us must become his own redeemer. But Jesus says *I can redeem you;* He alone can make that claim stick.

Acts 4:12 says, "No one else can save us. Indeed, we can be saved only by the power of the one named Jesus and not by any other person." There is salvation in no one else! God has given no other name under heaven by which we must be saved. That's what makes Jesus unique. Only He can save us from our sins.

To His disciples Jesus made the most audacious and exclusive statement ever made by a religious leader. He said, "I am the way, the truth, and the life. No one goes to the Father except through me" (John 14:6). No other person would even dare to make such a claim.

In *Simply Jesus*, you will encounter what the Gospel writers have to say about this most unique person—Jesus. You'll read their firsthand accounts of what they heard Him say and do. You'll travel with them to out-of-the-way places and walk with them in the company of Jesus. You'll read their private journals of their journey with Jesus, and you'll find many common points with your own journey with Him.

And if you've read the story of Jesus before and found it interesting but not unique—not life changing—then perhaps this time you'll go deeper. Perhaps this time you'll see more. Perhaps this time you'll discover the uniqueness of this Jesus of Nazareth. Perhaps this time, you won't just read history, you'll discover the way of eternal life.

Believing that Jesus died, that's history. Believing Jesus died for you, that's salvation. Look deeper and find your life in the life of Jesus.

Dr. Woodrow Kroll, president
Back to the Bible International
Lincoln, Nebraska

INTRODUCTION

> Once when Jesus was praying privately and his disciples were with him, he asked them, "Who do people say I am?" They answered, "Some say you are John the Baptizer, others Elijah, and still others say that one of the prophets from long ago has come back to life." He asked them, "But who do you say I am?" Peter answered, "You are the Messiah, whom God has sent." *~Luke 9:18–20*

Who do you say I am? That question has resounded throughout the ages. Who is Jesus? Holy man? Prophet? Teacher? Son of God? Every year a new crop of books and television documentaries appear, claiming to reveal the "real" truth about Jesus. Who are we to believe? Where do we turn for real answers to our doubts and questions?

The bottom line is that the single most significant piece of evidence we have regarding the life, death. and resurrection of Jesus is the Bible. Creative writers may be able to construct clever alternative versions of what they think really happened, but most of it is simply conjecture. If you want to know what Jesus really said, really did, and really claimed, you need to read the Bible. Whether or not you agree with it is a different matter, but the Bible is where you have to start.

Our hope is that this book will help you on this journey to discover who Jesus really is. We have taken the life and teachings of Jesus and arranged them chronologically in a simplified "harmony" of the four Gospel accounts. The goal is not to replace or somehow "improve" the canonical structure of the Gospels, but rather to present the elements of the life, death, and resurrection of Jesus in a clear chronological order. Where there are multiple accounts of the same event, we have included cross-references and encourage you to read the parallel accounts to see how they complement each other.

At the beginning of each section we have attempted to provide a brief introduction that summarizes the content and gives the reader a high-level overview. Interspersed with the biblical text we have included sidebars that provide historical context and application for certain key moments in the life and ministry of Jesus. These notes are designed to help the reader go a little deeper, giving him or her a model for bridging the gap from biblical text to current application.

My prayer is that as you read this book you, like Peter, will come to the same conclusion and will worship and proclaim Jesus as "the Messiah, whom God has sent."

—Jonathan Ziman

JESUS' COMING IS ANNOUNCED

Mark opens his Gospel with a combination of references from the Old Testament that ground his account firmly in God's promises of a Messiah. At the same time he foreshadows the coming of God's kingdom. With references to Isaiah 40, Malachi 3, and Exodus 23, Mark recalls for his readers the promise of restoration, the promise of hope after the long exile. However, before God himself can return, the people would first be granted opportunities to change the way they think and act. John the Baptizer is established here as the messenger who would prepare the way for the Lord. Thus Mark also makes clear for all his readers, at the very beginning of his Gospel, that Jesus is the Lord.

JOHN THE BAPTIZER PREPARES THE WAY
(MARK 1:1–8) *~see also Matthew 3:1–12; Luke 3:1–18; John 1:19–28~*

This is the beginning of the Good News about Jesus Christ, the Son of God. The prophet Isaiah wrote,

> "I am sending my messenger ahead of you
> to prepare the way for you."
> "A voice cries out in the desert:
> 'Prepare the way for the Lord!
> Make his paths straight!'"

John the Baptizer was in the desert telling people about a baptism of repentance for the forgiveness of sins. All Judea and all the people of Jerusalem went to him. As they confessed their sins, he baptized them in the Jordan River.

John was dressed in clothes made from camel's hair. He wore a leather belt around his waist and ate locusts and wild honey.

He announced, "The one who comes after me is more powerful than I. I am not worthy to bend down and untie his sandal straps. I have baptized you with water, but he will baptize you with the Holy Spirit."

LUKE WRITES TO THEOPHILUS (AROUND AD 60) TO TELL JESUS' STORY (LUKE 1:1–4)

Many have attempted to write about what had taken place among us. They received their information from those who had been eyewitnesses and servants of God's word from the beginning, and they passed it on to us. I, too, have followed everything closely from the beginning. So I thought it would be a good idea to write an orderly account for Your Excellency, Theophilus. In this way you will know that what you've been told is true.

JESUS' FORERUNNER, JOHN, IS BORN

For an audience and culture steeped in the Old Testament Scriptures, the events surrounding the birth of John are far more than just a nice parallel to the birth of Jesus. The temple in Jerusalem was the focal point of life and worship for the Jews, representing the presence of God in their midst. Envisioned by David, built by Solomon, destroyed in the exile, and fought for during the Maccabean revolt, the temple was the place where people looked for God to speak to them. However, after so many years of silence, even Zechariah was surprised when God did speak. Note also the powerful imagery of the barren woman, recalling the miraculous provision of God in the lives of Sarah, Rebekah, Rachel, and Hannah. Luke intentionally is drawing our attention to the fact that God is not just doing something special but something continuous with the Old Testament Scriptures.

AN ANGEL GABRIEL APPEARS TO ZECHARIAH (LUKE 1:5–25)

When Herod was king of Judea, there was a priest named Zechariah, who belonged to the division of priests named after Abijah. Zechariah's wife Elizabeth was a descendant of Aaron. Zechariah and Elizabeth had God's approval. They followed all the Lord's commands and regulations perfectly. Yet, they never had any children because Elizabeth couldn't become pregnant. Both of them were too old to have children.

Zechariah was on duty with his division of priests. As he served in God's presence, he was chosen by priestly custom to go into the Lord's temple to burn incense. All the people were praying outside while he was burning incense.

Then, to the right of the incense altar, an angel of the Lord appeared to him. Zechariah was troubled and overcome with fear.

The angel said to him, "Don't be afraid, Zechariah! God has heard your prayer. Your wife Elizabeth will have a son, and you will name him John. He will be your pride and joy, and many people will be glad that he was born. As far as the Lord is concerned, he will be a great man. He will never drink wine or any other liquor. He will be filled with the Holy Spirit even before he is born. He will bring many people in Israel back to the Lord their God. He will go ahead of the Lord with the spirit and power that Elijah had. He will change parents' attitudes toward their children. He will change disobedient people so that they will accept the wisdom of those who have God's approval. In this way he will prepare the people for their Lord."

Zechariah said to the angel, "What proof is there for this? I'm an old man, and my wife is beyond her childbearing years."

The angel answered him, "I'm Gabriel! I stand in God's presence. God sent me to tell you this good news. But because you didn't believe what I said, you will be unable to talk until the day this happens. Everything will come true at the right time."

Meanwhile, the people were waiting for Zechariah. They were amazed that he was staying in the temple so long. When he did come out, he was unable to speak to them. So they realized that he had seen a vision in the temple. He motioned to them but remained unable to talk.

When the days of his service were over, he went home. Later, his wife Elizabeth became pregnant and didn't go out in public for five months. She said, "The Lord has done this for me now. He has removed my public disgrace."

Your Wife Elizabeth Will Have a Son

Infertility is a theme that runs throughout the Scriptures, starting with Sarah (Genesis 18) and continuing with Rebekah (Genesis 25), Rachel (Genesis 30), the mother of Samson (Judges 13), Hannah (1 Samuel 1–2), and the Shunnamite woman (2 Kings 4). As Luke clearly points out regarding Elizabeth and Zechariah, the inability to conceive is never depicted as a punishment but rather provides an opportunity for God to display his power in bringing life where there is none—a foreshadowing of the true life Jesus would bring to a world dead in sin. The miracle of life in each of these cases emphasizes the corrupt state of the world, a place where humans now struggle to be fruitful and multiply (see Genesis 1:28). Yet, with the astonishing birth of John comes the realization that God is breaking into the world again, establishing through direct intervention a new direction and a new hope for the people of Israel.

THE ANGEL GABRIEL COMES TO MARY
(LUKE 1:26–38)

Six months after Elizabeth had become pregnant, God sent the angel Gabriel to Nazareth, a city in Galilee. The angel went to a virgin promised in marriage to a descendant of David named Joseph. The virgin's name was Mary.

When the angel entered her home, he greeted her and said, "You are favored by the Lord! The Lord is with you."

She was startled by what the angel said and tried to figure out what this greeting meant.

The angel told her,

> "Don't be afraid, Mary. You have found favor with God.
> You will become pregnant, give birth to a son,
>   and name him Jesus.
> He will be a great man
>   and will be called the Son of the Most High.
> The Lord God will give him
>   the throne of his ancestor David.
> Your son will be king of Jacob's people forever,
>   and his kingdom will never end."

Mary asked the angel, "How can this be? I've never had sexual intercourse."

The angel answered her, "The Holy Spirit will come to you, and the power of the Most High will overshadow you. Therefore, the holy child developing inside you will be called the Son of God.

"Elizabeth, your relative, is six months pregnant with a son in her old age. People said she couldn't have a child. But nothing is impossible for God."

Mary answered, "I am the Lord's servant. Let everything you've said happen to me."

Then the angel left her.

MARY VISITS ELIZABETH AND PRAISES GOD
(LUKE 1:39–56)

Soon afterward, Mary hurried to a city in the mountain region of Judah. She entered Zechariah's home and greeted Elizabeth.

When Elizabeth heard the greeting, she felt the baby kick. Elizabeth was filled with the Holy Spirit. She said in a loud voice, "You are the most blessed of all women, and blessed is the child that you will have. I feel blessed that the mother of my Lord is visiting me. As soon as I heard your greeting, I felt the baby jump for joy. You are blessed for believing that the Lord would keep his promise to you."

Mary said,

"My soul praises the Lord's greatness!
My spirit finds its joy in God, my Savior,
    because he has looked favorably on me, his humble servant.

"From now on, all people will call me blessed
    because the Almighty has done great things to me.
        His name is holy.
            For those who fear him,
                his mercy lasts throughout every generation.

"He displayed his mighty power.
    He scattered those who think too highly of themselves.
        He pulled strong rulers from their thrones.
            He honored humble people.
                He fed hungry people with good food.
                    He sent rich people away with nothing.

"He remembered to help his servant Israel forever.
    This is the promise he made to our ancestors,
        to Abraham and his descendants."

Mary stayed with Elizabeth about three months and then went back home.

The Magnificat

A young mother sings for joy at the new life in her womb, a child destined for astonishing glory and terrible suffering, a child who would be hailed as king and yet crucified as a common criminal. As theologian Clarice Martin has noted, Mary considers herself blessed not simply because she is pregnant but predominantly because she has been chosen by God to fulfill the promises he made long ago to "his servant Israel." (Joel B. Green, Scot McKnight, I. Howard Marshall, eds; *Dictionary of Jesus and the Gospels* [Downer's Grove, IL: InterVarsity Press, 1992], pp. 525-526.) Mary, a woman of low social standing and meager economic means, has been selected by God to play a key role. Her song is a joyous outburst of praise to God that the hope of redemption is now so near.

JOHN IS BORN
(LUKE 1:57–80)

When the time came for Elizabeth to have her child, she gave birth to a son. Her neighbors and relatives heard that the Lord had been very kind to her, and they shared her joy.

When the child was eight days old, they went to the temple to circumcise him. They were going to name him Zechariah after his father. But his mother spoke up, "Absolutely not! His name will be John."

Their friends said to her, "But you don't have any relatives with that name."

So they motioned to the baby's father to see what he wanted to name the child. Zechariah asked for a writing tablet and wrote, "His name is John." Everyone was amazed.

Suddenly, Zechariah was able to speak, and he began to praise God.

All their neighbors were filled with awe. Throughout the mountain region of Judea, people talked about everything that had happened. Everyone who heard about it seriously thought it over and asked, "What does the future hold for this child?" It was clear that the Lord was with him.

His father Zechariah was filled with the Holy Spirit and prophesied,

> "Praise the Lord God of Israel!
>> He has come to take care of his people
>>> and to set them free.
>> He has raised up a mighty Savior for us
>>> in the family of his servant David.
>> He made this promise through his holy prophets long ago.
>> He promised to save us from our enemies
>>> and from the power of all who hate us.
>> He has shown his mercy to our ancestors
>>> and remembered his holy promise,
>>>> the oath that he swore to our ancestor Abraham.
>> He promised to rescue us from our enemies' power
>>> so that we could serve him without fear
>>>> by being holy and honorable as long as we live.

> "You, child, will be called a prophet of the Most High.
> You will go ahead of the Lord to prepare his way.
> You will make his people know that they can be saved
>> through the forgiveness of their sins.

A new day will dawn on us from above
   because our God is loving and merciful.
He will give light to those who live in the dark
   and in death's shadow.
He will guide us into the way of peace."

The child John grew and became spiritually strong. He lived in the desert until the day he appeared to the people of Israel.

section three

JESUS IS BORN IN BETHLEHEM

The incarnation defies expectation and explanation. That the living God, the Creator of heaven and earth, the almighty and Holy One of Israel would take on human flesh is almost incomprehensible. Yet, it happened. And we stand in awe. Mary sang in praise. Joseph was humbled to obedience. While so many looked for a conquering king, a powerful restoration of God's presence among his people, in a quiet little village Jesus was born to ordinary parents in a humble setting. The prophetic promise of the coming day of the Lord dawned quietly, and hardly anyone noticed.

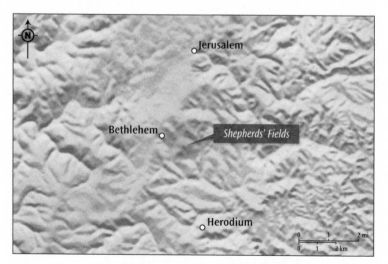

"Shepherds' Fields" Near Bethlehem

THE VIRGIN BIRTH OF JESUS
(MATTHEW 1:18–25)

The birth of Jesus Christ took place in this way. His mother Mary had been promised to Joseph in marriage. But before they were married, Mary realized that she was pregnant by the Holy Spirit. Her husband Joseph was an honorable man and did not want to disgrace her publicly. So he decided to break the marriage agreement with her secretly.

Joseph had this in mind when an angel of the Lord appeared to him in a dream. The angel said to him, "Joseph, descendant of David, don't be afraid to take Mary as your wife. She is pregnant by the Holy Spirit. She will give birth to a son, and you will name him Jesus [He Saves], because he will save his people from their sins." All this happened so that what the Lord had spoken through the prophet came true: "The virgin will become pregnant and give birth to a son, and they will name him Immanuel," which means "God is with us."

When Joseph woke up, he did what the angel of the Lord had commanded him to do. He took Mary to be his wife. He did not have marital relations with her before she gave birth to a son. Joseph named the child Jesus.

JESUS IS BORN AND ANGELS ANNOUNCE IT
(LUKE 2:1–20)

At that time the Emperor Augustus ordered a census of the Roman Empire. This was the first census taken while Quirinius was governor of Syria. All the people went to register in the cities where their ancestors had lived.

So Joseph went from Nazareth, a city in Galilee, to a Judean city called Bethlehem. Joseph, a descendant of King David, went to Bethlehem because David had been born there. Joseph went there to register with Mary. She had been promised to him in marriage and was pregnant.

While they were in Bethlehem, the time came for Mary to have her child. She gave birth to her firstborn son. She wrapped him in strips of cloth and laid him in a manger because there wasn't any room for them in the inn.

Shepherds were in the fields near Bethlehem. They were taking turns watching their flock during the night. An angel from the Lord suddenly appeared to them. The glory of the Lord filled the area with light, and they were terrified. The angel said to them, "Don't be afraid! I have good news for you, a message that will fill everyone with joy. Today your Savior, Christ the Lord, was born in David's city. This is how you will recognize him: You will find an infant wrapped in strips of cloth and lying in a manger."

Suddenly, a large army of angels appeared with the angel. They were praising God by saying,

> "Glory to God in the highest heaven,
> and on earth peace to those who have his good will!"

The angels left them and went back to heaven. The shepherds said to each other, "Let's go to Bethlehem and see what the Lord has told us about."

They went quickly and found Mary and Joseph with the baby, who was lying in a manger. When they saw the child, they repeated what they had been told about him. Everyone who heard the shepherds' story was amazed.

Mary treasured all these things in her heart and always thought about them.

As the shepherds returned to their flock, they glorified and praised God for everything they had seen and heard. Everything happened the way the angel had told them.

THE FAMILY LINE OF JESUS CHRIST
(MATTHEW 1:1–17)

This is the list of ancestors of Jesus Christ, descendant of David and Abraham.

> Abraham was the father of Isaac,
> Isaac the father of Jacob,
> Jacob the father of Judah and his brothers.
> Judah and Tamar were the father and mother of Perez and Zerah.
> Perez was the father of Hezron,
> Hezron the father of Ram,
> Ram the father of Amminadab,
> Amminadab the father of Nahshon,
> Nahshon the father of Salmon.
> Salmon and Rahab were the father and mother of Boaz.
> Boaz and Ruth were the father and mother of Obed.
> Obed was the father of Jesse,
> Jesse the father of King David.
> David and Uriah's wife Bathsheba were the father and mother of Solomon.
> Solomon was the father of Rehoboam,
> Rehoboam the father of Abijah,

Abijah the father of Asa,
Asa the father of Jehoshaphat,
Jehoshaphat the father of Joram,
Joram the father of Uzziah,
Uzziah the father of Jotham,
Jotham the father of Ahaz,
Ahaz the father of Hezekiah,
Hezekiah the father of Manasseh,
Manasseh the father of Amon,
Amon the father of Josiah.
Josiah was the father of Jechoniah and his brothers.
    They lived at the time when the people were exiled to Babylon.

After the exile to Babylon,

Jechoniah became the father of Shealtiel.
Shealtiel was the father of Zerubbabel,
Zerubbabel the father of Abiud,
Abiud the father of Eliakim,
Eliakim the father of Azor,
Azor the father of Zadok,
Zadok the father of Achim,
Achim the father of Eliud,
Eliud the father of Eleazar,
Eleazar the father of Matthan,
Matthan the father of Jacob.
Jacob was the father of Joseph, who was the husband of Mary.
    Mary was the mother of Jesus, who is called Christ.

So there were

14 generations from Abraham to David,
14 generations from David until the exile to Babylon,
14 generations from the exile until the Messiah.

THE WORD BECOMES HUMAN
(JOHN 1:1–18)

In the beginning the Word already existed. The Word was with God, and the Word was God. He was already with God in the beginning.

Everything came into existence through him. Not one thing that exists was made without him.

He was the source of life, and that life was the light for humanity.

The light shines in the dark, and the dark has never extinguished it.

God sent a man named John to be his messenger. John came to declare the truth about the light so that everyone would become believers through his message. John was not the light, but he came to declare the truth about the light.

The real light, which shines on everyone, was coming into the world. He was in the world, and the world came into existence through him. Yet, the world didn't recognize him. He went to his own people, and his own people didn't accept him. However, he gave the right to become God's children to everyone who believed in him. These people didn't become God's children in a physical way—from a human impulse or from a husband's desire to have a child. They were born from God.

The Word became human and lived among us. We saw his glory. It was the glory that the Father shares with his only Son, a glory full of kindness and truth.

(John declared the truth about him when he said loudly, "This is the person about whom I said, 'The one who comes after me was before me because he existed before I did.'")

Each of us has received one gift after another because of all that the Word is. The Teachings were given through Moses, but kindness and truth came into existence through Jesus Christ. No one has ever seen God. God's only Son, the one who is closest to the Father's heart, has made him known.

The Word Becomes Human

The first line of John's Gospel account makes a clear and obvious allusion to the opening line of Genesis. In doing so John boldly claims for his book a canonical status on a par with the most revered and well-established books of the Jewish faith. John alludes to the fact that just as Genesis recorded the creation of the world, his Gospel records the beginning of the new creation, a dominant theme among the Old Testament prophets. Finally, John's poetic prologue firmly establishes the divinity of Christ. Not only is Jesus God, but he is God *with us*. Jesus is the glory of God living and walking among his people, humbling himself in the form of a human in order to save his precious children (see Philippians 2:5–11).

JESUS GROWS UP IN NAZARETH

In place of the kind of biographical information we might wish to have about Jesus' childhood, Matthew and Luke use theologically charged language to describe the key events relating to his role as the chosen one. We read of his parents obedience to the Law in having Jesus circumcised and setting him "apart as holy to the Lord," foreshadowing the incredible life and ministry that lay ahead for Jesus. Some scholars see both here and throughout Luke's birth narrative a close parallel to the dedication and early childhood of Samuel, an Old Testament echo that highlights Jesus' elevated role as both priest and prophet. Meanwhile, the visit from the wise men emphasizes Jesus' role as king, the mighty ruler who deserves our worship—an early allusion to his divinity. Finally, the escape to Egypt recalls the powerful stories of the exodus and God's protection and provision for his people. The exodus was one of the most significant shaping events in Israel's history, and invoking that imagery here calls to mind the Passover and suggests the momentous events about to take place.

JESUS' PARENTS OBEY MOSES' TEACHINGS
(LUKE 2:21–24)

Eight days after his birth, the child was circumcised and named Jesus. This was the name the angel had given him before his mother became pregnant.

After the days required by Moses' Teachings to make a mother clean had passed, Joseph and Mary went to Jerusalem. They took Jesus to present him to the Lord. They did exactly what was written in the Lord's Teachings: "Every firstborn boy is to be set apart as holy to the Lord." They also offered a sacrifice as required by the Lord's Teachings: "a pair of mourning doves or two young pigeons."

SIMEON AND ANNA PROPHESY ABOUT JESUS
(LUKE 2:25–40)

A man named Simeon was in Jerusalem. He lived an honorable and devout life. He was waiting for the one who would comfort Israel. The Holy Spirit was with Simeon and had told him that he wouldn't die until he had seen the Messiah, whom the Lord would send.

Moved by the Spirit, Simeon went into the temple courtyard. Mary and Joseph were bringing the child Jesus into the courtyard at the same time. They brought him so that they could do for him what Moses' Teachings required. Then Simeon took the child in his arms and praised God by saying,

> "Now, Lord, you are allowing your servant to leave in peace as you
>   promised.
> My eyes have seen your salvation,
>   which you have prepared for all people to see.
>   He is a light that will reveal salvation to the nations
>   and bring glory to your people Israel."

Jesus' father and mother were amazed at what was said about him. Then Simeon blessed them and said to Mary, his mother, "This child is the reason that many people in Israel will be condemned and many others will be saved. He will be a sign that will expose the thoughts of those who reject him. And a sword will pierce your heart."

Anna, a prophet, was also there. She was a descendant of Phanuel from the tribe of Asher. She was now very old. Her husband had died seven years after they were married, and she had been a widow for 84 years. Anna never left the temple courtyard but worshiped day and night by fasting and praying. At that moment she came up to Mary and Joseph and began to thank God. She spoke about Jesus to all who were waiting for Jerusalem to be set free.

After doing everything the Lord's Teachings required, Joseph and Mary returned to their hometown of Nazareth in Galilee. The child grew and became strong. He was filled with wisdom, and God's favor was with him.

My Eyes Have Seen Your Salvation

Simeon's hymn of praise to God, often referred to as the *Nunc Dimittis,* is steeped in Old Testament language concerning the coming of God's kingdom. His comments are packed with allusions to prophecies from Isaiah regarding the coming Messiah and the salvation he would bring to Israel. Quite possibly building from images found in Isaiah 40, Simeon calls to mind a time of comfort and restoration for a people who have been scattered and live under foreign rule. Moreover, Simeon's song raises the possibility of salvation, including even those outside the traditional ethnic and religious boundaries of Judaism. Again, although this is drawn conceptually from passages in Isaiah, the expansion of the kingdom would be a stumbling block for many within the Jewish community, both throughout the life of Jesus and afterwards as the apostles took the gospel to the ends of the earth.

THE WISE MEN VISIT
(MATTHEW 2:1–12)

Jesus was born in Bethlehem in Judea when Herod was king. After Jesus' birth wise men from the east arrived in Jerusalem. They asked, "Where is the one who was born to be the king of the Jews? We saw his star rising and have come to worship him."

When King Herod and all Jerusalem heard about this, they became disturbed. He called together all the chief priests and scribes and tried to find out from them where the Messiah was supposed to be born.

They told him, "In Bethlehem in Judea. The prophet wrote about this:

Bethlehem in the land of Judah,
> you are by no means least among the leaders of Judah.
>> A leader will come from you.
>> He will shepherd my people Israel."

Then Herod secretly called the wise men and found out from them exactly when the star had appeared. As he sent them to Bethlehem, he said, "Go and search carefully for the child. When you have found him, report to me so that I may go and worship him too."

After they had heard the king, they started out. The star they had seen rising led them until it stopped over the place where the child was. They were overwhelmed with joy to see the star. When they entered the house, they saw the child with his mother Mary. So they bowed down and worshiped him. Then they opened their treasure chests and offered him gifts of gold, frankincense, and myrrh.

God warned them in a dream not to go back to Herod. So they left for their country by another road.

A True King

Herod the Great ruled Palestine from about 47 BC until shortly after the birth of Christ. Appointed as king by the Romans, Herod was actually only a half-Jew and was disliked by many. Although he did bring some element of peace and order to the country, he also raised taxes, both to keep the Romans happy and also to feed his own narcissistic building projects. He killed anyone who opposed him or threatened to oppose him, including several of his wives and children. In contrast to the extravagant power and wealth of Herod, Jesus, the true king of the Jews, was born in a humble and unassuming stable. In an astonishing reversal of expectations, when the wise men came from the east they largely ignored the evil Herod and instead brought their gifts to a baby in the insignificant town of Bethlehem.

ESCAPE TO EGYPT AND RETURN TO NAZARETH
(MATTHEW 2:13–23)

After they had left, an angel of the Lord appeared to Joseph in a dream. The angel said to him, "Get up, take the child and his mother, and flee to Egypt. Stay there until I tell you, because Herod intends to search for the child and kill him."

Joseph got up, took the child and his mother, and left for Egypt that night. He stayed there until Herod died. What the Lord had spoken through the prophet came true: "I have called my son out of Egypt."

When Herod saw that the wise men had tricked him, he became furious. He sent soldiers to kill all the boys two years old and younger in or near Bethlehem. This matched the exact time he had learned from the wise men. Then the words spoken through the prophet Jeremiah came true:

> "A sound was heard in Ramah,
>> the sound of crying in bitter grief.
>>> Rachel was crying for her children.
>>> She refused to be comforted
>>>> because they were dead."

After Herod was dead, an angel of the Lord appeared in a dream to Joseph in Egypt. The angel said to him, "Get up, take the child and his mother, and go to Israel. Those who tried to kill the child are dead."

Joseph got up, took the child and his mother, and went to Israel. But when he heard that Archelaus had succeeded his father Herod as king of Judea, Joseph was afraid to go there. Warned in a dream, he left for Galilee and made his home in a city called Nazareth. So what the prophets had said came true: "He will be called a Nazarene."

MARY AND JOSEPH FIND JESUS WITH THE TEACHERS IN THE TEMPLE COURTYARD
(LUKE 2:41–52)

Every year Jesus' parents would go to Jerusalem for the Passover festival. When he was 12 years old, they went as usual.

When the festival was over, they left for home. The boy Jesus stayed behind in Jerusalem, but his parents didn't know it. They thought that he was with the others who were traveling with them. After traveling for a day, they started to look for him among their relatives and friends. When they didn't find him, they went back to Jerusalem to look for him.

Three days later, they found him in the temple courtyard. He was sitting among the teachers, listening to them, and asking them questions. His understanding and his answers stunned everyone who heard him.

When his parents saw him, they were shocked. His mother asked him, "Son, why have you done this to us? Your father and I have been worried sick looking for you!"

Jesus said to them, "Why were you looking for me? Didn't you realize that I had to be in my Father's house?" But they didn't understand what he meant.

Then he returned with them to Nazareth and was obedient to them.

His mother treasured all these things in her heart. Jesus grew in wisdom and maturity. He gained favor from God and people.

JESUS PREPARES FOR HIS MINISTRY

It is sometimes hard to imagine a world where Jesus is not a household name. A place where there are no stereotyped images of what Jesus looks like and nobody calls themselves a Christian. Yet, this was the world John the Baptizer and the first disciples lived in. Although many people were

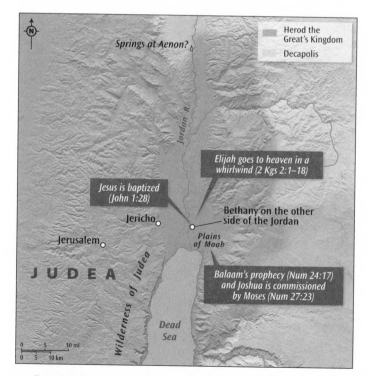

Jesus' Baptism at Bethany on the Other Side of the Jordan

hopeful the Messiah would come soon, probably few of them expected he would actually show up in their hometown. Some, however, clearly were paying more attention than others. John the Baptizer, Andrew, Simon Peter, Philip, and Nathanael instantly followed "the Lamb of God" while many of the Pharisees and religious leaders were so angered by John's call to repentance that they couldn't see the Savior standing right in front of them.

JOHN PREPARES THE WAY
(MATTHEW 3:1–12) ~see also Mark 1:1–8; Luke 3:1–18; John 1:19–28~

Later, John the Baptizer appeared in the desert of Judea. His message was, "Turn to God and change the way you think and act, because the kingdom of heaven is near." Isaiah the prophet spoke about this man when he said,

> "A voice cries out in the desert:
> 'Prepare the way for the Lord!
> Make his paths straight!'"

John wore clothes made from camel's hair and had a leather belt around his waist. His diet consisted of locusts and wild honey.

Jerusalem, all Judea, and the whole Jordan Valley went to him. As they confessed their sins, he baptized them in the Jordan River.

But when he saw many Pharisees and Sadducees coming to be baptized, he said to them, "You poisonous snakes! Who showed you how to flee from God's coming anger? Do those things that prove you have turned to God and have changed the way you think and act. Don't think you can say, 'Abraham is our ancestor.' I can guarantee that God can raise up descendants for Abraham from these stones. The ax is now ready to cut the roots of the trees. Any tree that doesn't produce good fruit will be cut down and thrown into a fire. I baptize you with water so that you will change the way you think and act. But the one who comes after me is more powerful than I. I am not worthy to remove his sandals. He will baptize you with the Holy Spirit and fire. His winnowing shovel is in his hand, and he will clean up his threshing floor. He will gather his wheat into a barn, but he will burn the husks in a fire that can never be put out."

JOHN BAPTIZES JESUS
(MATTHEW 3:13–17) ~see also Mark 1:9–11; Luke 3:21–22~

Then Jesus appeared. He came from Galilee to the Jordan River to be baptized by John. But John tried to stop him and said, "I need to be baptized by you. Why are you coming to me?"

Jesus answered him, "This is the way it has to be now. This is the proper way to do everything that God requires of us."

Then John gave in to him. After Jesus was baptized, he immediately came up from the water. Suddenly, the heavens were opened, and he saw the Spirit of God coming down as a dove to him. Then a voice from heaven said, "This is my Son, whom I love—my Son with whom I am pleased."

Jesus' Baptism

It seems odd to some that the man who claimed to be God should have submitted himself to baptism, a rite which, at the time, symbolized repentance for sin (Mark 1:4). However, while Jesus was without sin and therefore had no need for personal repentance, the focus here is on obedience to the will of God. Jesus ignores John's hesitancy because Jesus knows this is the time God has ordained for him to be baptized, a fact confirmed by the miraculous events that follow. The moment of obedience became a moment of blessing and pronouncement, a public declaration of God's power and authority invested in his Son. At this crucial moment near the beginning of his ministry, the baptism proved to be a critical test of Jesus' obedience and willingness to submit.

THE DEVIL TEMPTS JESUS
(LUKE 4:1–13) ~see also Matthew 4:1–11; Mark 1:12–13~

Jesus was filled with the Holy Spirit as he left the Jordan River. The Spirit led him while he was in the desert, where he was tempted by the devil for 40 days. During those days Jesus ate nothing, so when they were over, he was hungry.

The devil said to him, "If you are the Son of God, tell this stone to become a loaf of bread."

Jesus answered him, "Scripture says, 'A person cannot live on bread alone.'"

The devil took him to a high place and showed him all the kingdoms of the world in an instant. The devil said to him, "I will give you all the power and glory of these kingdoms. All of it has been given to me, and I give it to anyone I please. So if you will worship me, all this will be yours."

Jesus answered him, "Scripture says, 'Worship the Lord your God and serve only him.'"

Then the devil took him into Jerusalem and had him stand on the highest part of the temple. He said to Jesus, "If you are the Son of God, jump from here! Scripture says, 'He will put his angels in charge of you to watch over you carefully. They will carry you in their hands so that you never hit your foot against a rock.'"

Jesus answered him, "It has been said, 'Never tempt the Lord your God.'"

After the devil had finished tempting Jesus in every possible way, the devil left him until another time.

JOHN IDENTIFIES JESUS AS THE LAMB OF GOD
(JOHN 1:19–34) ~see also Matthew 3:1–12; Mark 1:1–8; Luke 3:1–18~

This was John's answer when the Jews sent priests and Levites from Jerusalem to ask him, "Who are you?" John didn't refuse to answer. He told them clearly, "I'm not the Messiah."

They asked him, "Well, are you Elijah?"

John answered, "No, I'm not."

Then they asked, "Are you the prophet?"

John replied, "No."

So they asked him, "Who are you? Tell us so that we can take an answer back to those who sent us. What do you say about yourself?"

John said, "I'm a voice crying out in the desert, 'Make the way for the Lord straight,' as the prophet Isaiah said."

Some of those who had been sent were Pharisees. They asked John, "Why do you baptize if you're not the Messiah or Elijah or the prophet?"

John answered them, "I baptize with water. Someone you don't know is standing among you. He's the one who comes after me. I am not worthy to untie his sandal strap."

This happened in Bethany on the east side of the Jordan River, where John was baptizing.

John saw Jesus coming toward him the next day and said, "Look! This is the Lamb of God who takes away the sin of the world. He is the one I spoke about when I said, 'A man who comes after me was before me because he existed before I did.' I didn't know who he was. However, I came to baptize with water to show him to the people of Israel."

John said, "I saw the Spirit come down as a dove from heaven and stay on him. I didn't know who he was. But God, who sent me to baptize with water, had told me, 'When you see the Spirit come down and stay on someone, you'll know that person is the one who baptizes with the Holy Spirit.' I have seen this and have declared that this is the Son of God."

CALLING OF THE FIRST DISCIPLES
(JOHN 1:35–51)

The next day John was standing with two of his disciples. John saw Jesus walk by. John said, "Look! This is the Lamb of God." When the two disciples heard John say this, they followed Jesus.

Jesus turned around and saw them following him. He asked them, "What are you looking for?"

They said to him, "Rabbi" (which means "teacher"), "where are you staying?"

Jesus told them, "Come, and you will see." So they went to see where he was staying and spent the rest of that day with him. It was about ten o'clock in the morning.

Andrew, Simon Peter's brother, was one of the two disciples who heard John and followed Jesus. Andrew at once found his brother Simon and told him, "We have found the Messiah" (which means "Christ"). Andrew brought Simon to Jesus.

Jesus looked at Simon and said, "You are Simon, son of John. Your name will be Cephas" (which means "Peter").

The next day Jesus wanted to go to Galilee. He found Philip and told him, "Follow me!" (Philip was from Bethsaida, the hometown of Andrew and Peter.)

Philip found Nathanael and told him, "We have found the man whom Moses wrote about in his teachings and whom the prophets wrote about. He is Jesus, son of Joseph, from the city of Nazareth."

Nathanael said to Philip, "Can anything good come from Nazareth?"

Philip told him, "Come and see!"

Jesus saw Nathanael coming toward him and remarked, "Here is a true Israelite who is sincere."

Nathanael asked Jesus, "How do you know anything about me?"

Jesus answered him, "I saw you under the fig tree before Philip called you."

Nathanael said to Jesus, "Rabbi, you are the Son of God! You are the king of Israel!"

Jesus replied, "You believe because I told you that I saw you under the fig tree. You will see greater things than that." Jesus said to Nathanael, "I can guarantee this truth: You will see the sky open and God's angels going up and coming down to the Son of Man."

JESUS BEGINS HIS MINISTRY IN CANA

This well known yet frequently misunderstood miracle is a fascinating example both of Jesus' divine power and his status as the Messiah. Commentators have noted that throughout the Old Testament the dawning of the messianic kingdom is symbolized using the imagery of an abundance of wine. Clearly, then, Jesus was not trying to make a point about alcohol consumption or wedding parties. This was a deliberate act meant to contrast the emptiness of the Jewish purification rituals with the fullness of life that Jesus was about to offer. It was also a clear demonstration of Jesus' divine power over creation, recalling the creative powers of God displayed in the opening chapters of Genesis.

JESUS CHANGES WATER INTO WINE
(JOHN 2:1–12)

Three days later a wedding took place in the city of Cana in Galilee. Jesus' mother was there. Jesus and his disciples had been invited too.

When the wine was gone, Jesus' mother said to him, "They're out of wine."

Jesus said to her, "Why did you come to me? My time has not yet come."

His mother told the servers, "Do whatever he tells you."

Six stone water jars were there. They were used for Jewish purification rituals. Each jar held 18 to 27 gallons.

Jesus told the servers, "Fill the jars with water." The servers filled the jars to the brim. Jesus said to them, "Pour some, and take it to the person in charge." The servers did as they were told.

The person in charge tasted the water that had become wine. He didn't know where it had come from, although the servers who had poured the water knew. The person in charge called the groom and said to him, "Everyone serves the best wine first. When people are drunk, the host serves cheap wine. But you have saved the best wine for now."

Cana in Galilee was the place where Jesus began to perform miracles. He made his glory public there, and his disciples believed in him.

After this, Jesus, his mother, brothers, and disciples went to the city of Capernaum and stayed there for a few days.

Miracles and Ministry

The ministry of Jesus was marked by many miracles, but what purpose did they serve? First and foremost, the miracles showed Jesus' divinely appointed power and authority. There were miracles that showed his power over creation, over human sickness, over spiritual oppression, and ultimately over the death-grip of sin. Second, God's heart breaks at the sight of a world corrupted by the evil effects of sin, and he rejoices to see his people and his creation restored, even in little ways. Although Jesus' primary mission was spiritual redemption, along the way he delighted to bring to his people a foretaste of the kind of global physical redemption we shall enjoy in the new heaven and the new earth.

JESUS TRAVELS TO JERUSALEM

The powerful scene of Jesus clearing the temple courtyard calls to mind for the disciples Psalm 69:9, yet almost immediately it becomes clear that Jesus is not primarily concerned with cleansing or rededicating the temple. Rather, he is preparing the people for his own death and resurrection—God's rescue plan for all of humanity. Jesus' plans are to reach the entire world, as he would soon explain to an incredulous and somewhat confused Jewish Pharisee named Nicodemus.

JESUS THROWS MERCHANTS AND MONEYCHANGERS OUT OF THE TEMPLE COURTYARD
(JOHN 2:13–25)

The Jewish Passover was near, so Jesus went to Jerusalem. He found those who were selling cattle, sheep, and pigeons in the temple courtyard. He also found moneychangers sitting there. He made a whip from small ropes and threw everyone with their sheep and cattle out of the temple courtyard. He dumped the moneychangers' coins and knocked over their tables.

He told those who sold pigeons, "Pick up this stuff, and get it out of here! Stop making my Father's house a marketplace!"

His disciples remembered that Scripture said, "Devotion for your house will consume me."

The Jews reacted by asking Jesus, "What miracle can you show us to justify what you're doing?"

Jesus replied, "Tear down this temple, and I'll rebuild it in three days."

The Jews said, "It took forty-six years to build this temple. Do you really think you're going to rebuild it in three days?"

But the temple Jesus spoke about was his own body. After he came back to life, his disciples remembered that he had said this. So they believed the Scripture and this statement that Jesus had made.

While Jesus was in Jerusalem at the Passover festival, many people believed in him because they saw the miracles that he performed. Jesus, however, was wary of these believers. He understood people and didn't need anyone to tell him about human nature. He knew what people were really like.

A Temple Tantrum

Jesus did not come to "clean up" the current worship practices of the Jews, he came to establish an entirely new system of belief, with himself at the center. The disciples recognized in his actions an allusion to Psalm 69:9, calling to mind King David, from whose line everyone knew would one day come the Messiah. Moreover, there was an expectation that this Messiah would purify the temple and restore true worship of God in Israel. Jesus awakened these thoughts in the people, but then subverted their assumptions and instead revealed his true purpose—the death and resurrection that would lead to true worship of him as Lord.

A CONVERSATION WITH NICODEMUS
(JOHN 3:1–21)

Nicodemus was a Pharisee and a member of the Jewish council. He came to Jesus one night and said to him, "Rabbi, we know that God has sent you as a teacher. No one can perform the miracles you perform unless God is with him."

Jesus replied to Nicodemus, "I can guarantee this truth: No one can see the kingdom of God without being born from above."

Nicodemus asked him, "How can anyone be born when he's an old man? He can't go back inside his mother a second time to be born, can he?"

Jesus answered Nicodemus, "I can guarantee this truth: No one can enter the kingdom of God without being born of water and the Spirit. Flesh and blood give birth to flesh and blood, but the Spirit gives birth to things that are spiritual. Don't be surprised when I tell you that all of you must be born from above. The wind blows wherever it pleases. You hear its sound, but you don't know where the wind comes from or where it's going. That's the way it is with everyone born of the Spirit."

Nicodemus replied, "How can that be?"

Jesus told Nicodemus, "You're a well-known teacher of Israel. Can't you understand this? I can guarantee this truth: We know what we're talking about, and we confirm what we've seen. Yet, you don't accept our message. If you don't believe me when I tell you about things on earth, how will you believe me when I tell you about things in heaven? No one has gone to heaven except the Son of Man, who came from heaven.

"As Moses lifted up the snake on a pole in the desert, so the Son of Man must be lifted up. Then everyone who believes in him will have eternal life."

God loved the world this way: He gave his only Son so that everyone who believes in him will not die but will have eternal life. God sent his Son into the world, not to condemn the world, but to save the world. Those who believe in him won't be condemned. But those who don't believe are already condemned because they don't believe in God's only Son.

This is why people are condemned: The light came into the world. Yet, people loved the dark rather than the light because their actions were evil. People who do what is wrong hate the light and don't come to the light. They don't want their actions to be exposed. But people who do what is true come to the light so that the things they do for God may be clearly seen.

Conversion: A Spiritual Rebirth

Young and old people alike are fully aware that being born again is physically impossible. Yet Jesus admonishes Nicodemus for failing to understand the allusion to a new beginning, a clean slate, a heart washed clean. Through the prophets' messages, God had sprinkled promises of a fresh start for his people that would mark the arrival of his Messiah among us. Although Israel had strayed far away from him, God promised that he would work to draw them back to himself. This is the imagery Jesus uses here—that new life is initiated and sustained by the power of the Holy Spirit, God working in us according to his plans and purposes.

JOHN THE BAPTIZER TALKS ABOUT CHRIST
(JOHN 3:22–36)

Later, Jesus and his disciples went to the Judean countryside, where he spent some time with them and baptized people. John was baptizing in Aenon, near Salim. Water was plentiful there. (People came to John to be baptized, since John had not yet been put in prison.)

Some of John's disciples had an argument with a Jew about purification ceremonies. So they went to John and asked him, "Rabbi, do you remember the man you spoke so favorably about when he was with you on the other side of the Jordan River? Well, he's baptizing, and everyone is going to him!"

John answered, "People can't receive anything unless it has been given to them from heaven. You are witnesses that I said, 'I'm not the Messiah, but I've been sent ahead of him.'

"The groom is the person to whom the bride belongs. The best man, who stands and listens to him, is overjoyed when the groom speaks. This is the joy that I feel. He must increase in importance, while I must decrease in importance.

"The person who comes from above is superior to everyone. I, a person from the earth, know nothing but what is on earth, and that's all I can talk about. The person who comes from heaven is superior to everyone and tells what he has seen and heard. Yet, no one accepts what he says. I have accepted what that person said, and I have affirmed that God is truthful. The man whom God has sent speaks God's message. After all, God gives him the Spirit without limit. The Father loves his Son and has put everything in his power. Whoever believes in the Son has eternal life, but whoever rejects the Son will not see life. Instead, he will see God's constant anger."

The Good News (John 3:16)

Familiarity with a verse can cause us to miss the amazing claim imbedded in it. In John 3:16 we see the fulfillment of a promise alluded to in Genesis 3:15. When Adam and Eve committed the first sin, God removed them from the garden. Yet he left them the hint of a time when Satan would be crushed forever. Here Jesus announces the amazing details of that divine rescue plan—that the depth of God's love for the world would lead him to offer his Son as the ultimate sacrifice, paying the debt once and for all and permanently ending Satan's hold on our lives.

HEROD PUTS JOHN THE BAPTIZER IN PRISON
(LUKE 3:19–20)

John spoke out against the ruler Herod because Herod had married his own sister-in-law, Herodias. He also spoke out against Herod for all the evil things he had done. So Herod added one more evil to all the others; he locked John in prison.

Eternal Life (John 3:15–18)

The eternal life promised by Jesus is contrasted with the new lease on life assured to the people who looked at the snake Moses held up in the desert. However, the contrast is expanded upon by Jesus. Just as the Israelites received physical healing and new life, those who put their faith and trust in Jesus would receive spiritual healing, redemption of sins, and entrance into eternal life. The promise was not just surprising, it was shocking. Who could make a promise like that? What would it even mean to have eternal life? The only other person who knows eternity is God, and so to experience eternal life would mean to be forever in the presence of God. Nicodemus could hardly make sense of it, and with a strange kind of irony, this very offer of eternal life would lead in part to Jesus' death.

JESUS VISITS SAMARIA

Jesus' parting command to the disciples as recorded in Acts 1:8 includes the surprising twist that they were to take the gospel even to Samaria. The disciples shouldn't have been surprised, for even early on in his ministry Jesus reached out across cultural and religious divides to touch the heart of a Samaritan woman deeply enmeshed in sin. His gentle, yet probing

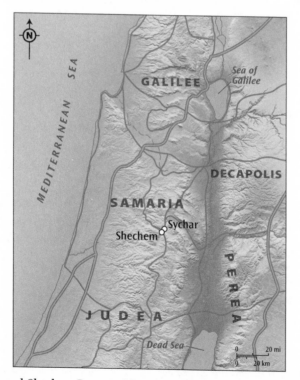

Sychar and Shechem Between Mountains Ebal and Gerizim in Samaria

and ultimately challenging response to her questions led not just to her conversion but also to many other Samaritans believing in Jesus. The irony is that while Jesus was offering the woman the true, living water, his own disciples couldn't see beyond their own physical needs for food and drink.

A SAMARITAN WOMAN MEETS JESUS AT A WELL
(JOHN 4:1–42)

Jesus knew that the Pharisees had heard that he was making and baptizing more disciples than John. (Actually, Jesus was not baptizing people. His disciples were.) So he left the Judean countryside and went back to Galilee.

Jesus had to go through Samaria. He arrived at a city in Samaria called Sychar. Sychar was near the piece of land that Jacob had given to his son Joseph. Jacob's Well was there. Jesus sat down by the well because he was tired from traveling. The time was about six o'clock in the evening.

A Samaritan woman went to get some water. Jesus said to her, "Give me a drink of water." (His disciples had gone into the city to buy some food.)

The Samaritan woman asked him, "How can a Jewish man like you ask a Samaritan woman like me for a drink of water?" (Jews, of course, don't associate with Samaritans.)

Jesus replied to her, "If you only knew what God's gift is and who is asking you for a drink, you would have asked him for a drink. He would have given you living water."

The woman said to him, "Sir, you don't have anything to use to get water, and the well is deep. So where are you going to get this living water? You're not more important than our ancestor Jacob, are you? He gave us this well. He and his sons and his animals drank water from it."

Jesus answered her, "Everyone who drinks this water will become thirsty again. But those who drink the water that I will give them will never become thirsty again. In fact, the water I will give them will become in them a spring that gushes up to eternal life."

The woman told Jesus, "Sir, give me this water! Then I won't get thirsty or have to come here to get water."

Jesus told her, "Go to your husband, and bring him here."

The woman replied, "I don't have a husband."

Jesus told her, "You're right when you say that you don't have a husband. You've had five husbands, and the man you have now isn't your husband. You've told the truth."

The woman said to Jesus, "I see that you're a prophet! Our ancestors worshiped on this mountain. But you Jews say that people must worship in Jerusalem."

Jesus told her, "Believe me. A time is coming when you Samaritans won't be worshiping the Father on this mountain or in Jerusalem. You don't know what you're worshiping. We Jews know what we're worshiping, because salvation comes from the Jews. Indeed, the time is coming, and it is now here, when the true worshipers will worship the Father in spirit and truth. The Father is looking for people like that to worship him. God is a spirit. Those who worship him must worship in spirit and truth."

The woman said to him, "I know that the Messiah is coming. When he comes, he will tell us everything." (*Messiah* is the one called *Christ*.)

Jesus told her, "I am he, and I am speaking to you now."

At that time his disciples returned. They were surprised that he was talking to a woman. But none of them asked him, "What do you want from her?" or "Why are you talking to her?"

Then the woman left her water jar and went back into the city. She told the people, "Come with me, and meet a man who told me everything I've ever done. Could he be the Messiah?" The people left the city and went to meet Jesus.

Meanwhile, the disciples were urging him, "Rabbi, have something to eat."

Jesus told them, "I have food to eat that you don't know about."

The disciples asked each other, "Did someone bring him something to eat?"

Jesus told them, "My food is to do what the one who sent me wants me to do and to finish the work he has given me.

"Don't you say, 'In four more months the harvest will be here'? I'm telling you to look and see that the fields are ready to be harvested. The person who harvests the crop is already getting paid. He is gathering grain for eternal life. So the person who plants the grain and the person who harvests it are happy together. In this respect the saying is true: 'One person plants, and another person harvests.' I have sent you to harvest a crop you have not worked for. Other people have done the hard work, and you have followed them in their work."

Many Samaritans in that city believed in Jesus because of the woman who said, "He told me everything I've ever done." So when the Samaritans went to Jesus, they asked him to stay with them. He stayed in Samaria for two days. Many more Samaritans believed because of what Jesus said. They told the woman, "Our faith is no longer based on what you've said. We have heard him ourselves, and we know that he really is the savior of the world."

The Jewish/Samaritan Schism

How could two people groups living so close to each other and sharing so many similarities be so antagonistic toward each other? The precise source of the schism is hard to pinpoint. Some trace the roots back to the time when the center of worship was moved from Mount Gerizim to Jerusalem. Others claim that the Samaritans were descended from colonizers imported by the Assyrians during the exile. Whatever the ancient history, in about 120–110 BC, the Hasmonean king John Hyrcanus went on a campaign to expand the territory of Judea and in the process destroyed the town of Shechem and burned down their center of worship on Mount Gerizim. From this point on it was hard for the Jews and Samaritans to find much common ground.

JESUS PREACHES IN GALILEE

A rich agricultural land bordering a large lake. Fishing villages bustling with activity. A checkered history as part of the exiled Northern Kingdom of Israel. Re-populated with Gentiles but mostly Jewish at the time of Jesus, Galilee was at the heart of Jesus' ministry. Traveling from town to town preaching the Good News, healing people and performing miracles, Jesus reached out to everyday people who were far removed from the religious and cultural center of Jerusalem. His ministry is filled with allusions to Old Testament prophecies about the Messiah, yet even so, most people fail to grasp the eternal significance of his actions.

A LIGHT HAS RISEN
(MATTHEW 4:12–17)

When Jesus heard that John had been put in prison, he went back to Galilee. He left Nazareth and made his home in Capernaum on the shores of the Sea of Galilee. This was in the region of Zebulun and Naphtali. So what the prophet Isaiah had said came true:

> "Land of Zebulun and land of Naphtali,
>   on the way to the sea,
>   across the Jordan River,
>   Galilee, where foreigners live!
> The people who lived in darkness
>   have seen a bright light.

A light has risen
for those who live in a land overshadowed by death."

From then on, Jesus began to tell people, "Turn to God and change the way you think and act, because the kingdom of heaven is near!"

A BELIEVING OFFICIAL
(JOHN 4:43–54) ~see also Matthew 8:5–13; Luke 7:1–10~

After spending two days in Samaria, Jesus left for Galilee. Jesus had said that a prophet is not honored in his own country. But when Jesus arrived in Galilee, the people of Galilee welcomed him. They had seen everything he had done at the festival in Jerusalem, since they, too, had attended the festival.

Jesus returned to the city of Cana in Galilee, where he had changed water into wine. A government official was in Cana. His son was sick in Capernaum. The official heard that Jesus had returned from Judea to Galilee. So he went to Jesus and asked him to go to Capernaum with him to heal his son who was about to die.

Jesus told the official, "If people don't see miracles and amazing things, they won't believe."

The official said to him, "Sir, come with me before my little boy dies."

Jesus told him, "Go home. Your son will live." The man believed what Jesus told him and left.

While the official was on his way to Capernaum, his servants met him and told him that his boy was alive. The official asked them at what time his son got better. His servants told him, "The fever left him yesterday evening at seven o'clock." Then the boy's father realized that it was the same time that Jesus had told him, "Your son will live." So the official and his entire family became believers.

This was the second miracle that Jesus performed after he had come back from Judea to Galilee.

NAZARETH REJECTS JESUS
(LUKE 4:14–30) ~see also Matthew 13:54–58; Mark 6:1–6~

Jesus returned to Galilee. The power of the Spirit was with him, and the news about him spread throughout the surrounding country. He taught in the synagogues, and everyone praised him.

Then Jesus came to Nazareth, where he had been brought up. As usual he went into the synagogue on the day of worship. He stood up to read the lesson. The attendant gave him the book of the prophet Isaiah. He opened it and found the place where it read:

"The Spirit of the Lord is with me.
He has anointed me
to tell the Good News to the poor.
He has sent me
to announce forgiveness to the prisoners of sin
and the restoring of sight to the blind,
to forgive those who have been shattered by sin,
to announce the year of the Lord's favor."

Jesus closed the book, gave it back to the attendant, and sat down. Everyone in the synagogue watched him closely. Then he said to them, "This passage came true today when you heard me read it."

All the people spoke well of him. They were amazed to hear the gracious words flowing from his lips. They said, "Isn't this Joseph's son?"

So he said to them, "You'll probably quote this proverb to me, 'Doctor, cure yourself!' and then say to me, 'Do all the things in your hometown that we've heard you've done in Capernaum.'" Then Jesus added, "I can guarantee this truth: A prophet isn't accepted in his hometown.

"I can guarantee this truth: There were many widows in Israel in Elijah's time. It had not rained for three-and-a-half years, and the famine was severe everywhere in the country. But God didn't send Elijah to anyone except a widow at Zarephath in the territory of Sidon. There were also many people with skin diseases in Israel in the prophet Elisha's time. But God cured no one except Naaman from Syria."

Everyone in the synagogue became furious when they heard this. Their city was built on a hill with a cliff. So they got up, forced Jesus out of the city, and led him to the cliff. They intended to throw him off of it. But Jesus walked right by them and went away.

"The Spirit of the Lord Is with Me"

The book of Isaiah was perhaps the most widely read and best known of all the prophetic literature at the time of Jesus. Allusions to and association with the text were commonplace among rabbis and teachers of the Law. In this passage from Isaiah 61, the clear message is that although judgment had been passed on Israel, a day would come when all would be made right again. This was a clear and profoundly important message for the people of Isaiah's time, yet it also came to have messianic overtones by the time of Jesus. In reading this passage and claiming to be its fulfillment, Jesus not only placed himself in the position of mouthpiece for God but also assumed the position of God as well. Jesus was not merely, as Isaiah did, prophesying about what would happen one day; Jesus claimed that he himself was the fulfillment of the prophecy. The claim was, of course, absolutely true, although it was too incredible for the people to believe, and they tried to throw him off a cliff for his blasphemy.

CALLING OF THE FIRST DISCIPLES
(MARK 1:14–20) ~see also Matthew 4:18–22; Luke 5:1–11~

After John had been put in prison, Jesus went to Galilee and told people the Good News of God. He said, "The time has come, and the kingdom of God is near. Change the way you think and act, and believe the Good News."

As he was going along the Sea of Galilee, he saw Simon and his brother Andrew. They were throwing a net into the sea because they were fishermen. Jesus said to them, "Come, follow me! I will teach you how to catch people instead of fish." They immediately left their nets and followed him.

As Jesus went on a little farther, he saw James and John, the sons of Zebedee. They were in a boat preparing their nets to go fishing. He immediately called them, and they left their father Zebedee and the hired men in the boat and followed Jesus.

JESUS FORCES AN EVIL SPIRIT OUT OF A MAN
(MARK 1:21–28) ~see also Luke 4:31–37~

Then they went to Capernaum. On the next day of worship, Jesus went into the synagogue and began to teach. The people were amazed at his teachings. Unlike their scribes, he taught them with authority.

At that time there was a man in the synagogue who was controlled by an evil spirit. He shouted, "What do you want with us, Jesus from Nazareth? Have you come to destroy us? I know who you are—the Holy One of God!"

Jesus ordered the spirit, "Keep quiet, and come out of him!" The evil spirit threw the man into convulsions and came out of him with a loud shriek.

Everyone was stunned. They said to each other, "What is this? This is a new teaching that has authority behind it! He gives orders to evil spirits, and they obey him."

The news about him spread quickly throughout the surrounding region of Galilee.

The Holy One of God

Everywhere Jesus went he confronted people with the challenge of deciding who he was. Clearly more than just another teacher, not living like John the Baptizer, not part of the Jerusalem religious elite, and imbued with astonishing power, Jesus caused a stir wherever he went. Yet, while many people were confused as to his true identity, the dark spiritual forces of the world knew exactly who he was and trembled (James 2:19). They knew that he was sent from God and that his presence could only mean their imminent destruction. Contrary to popular culture, which presents God and the devil as equal and opposite forces battling it out for victory, the biblical witness is clear that the Holy One alone is sovereign, and the demons have nothing to stand on.

JESUS CURES SIMON'S MOTHER-IN-LAW AND MANY OTHERS
(MARK 1:29–34) ~see also Matthew 8:14–18; Luke 4:38–41~

After they left the synagogue, they went directly to the house of Simon and Andrew. James and John went with them. Simon's mother-in-law was in bed with a fever. The first thing they did was to tell Jesus about her. Jesus went to her, took her hand, and helped her get up. The fever went away, and she prepared a meal for them.

In the evening, when the sun had set, people brought to him everyone who was sick and those possessed by demons. The whole city had gathered at his door. He cured many who were sick with various diseases and forced many demons out of people. However, he would not allow the demons to speak. After all, they knew who he was.

SPREADING THE GOOD NEWS IN GALILEE
(MARK 1:35–39) ~see also Matthew 4:23–25; Luke 4:42–44~

In the morning, long before sunrise, Jesus went to a place where he could be alone to pray. Simon and his friends searched for him. When they found him, they told him, "Everyone is looking for you."

Jesus said to them, "Let's go somewhere else, to the small towns that are nearby. I have to spread the Good News in them also. This is why I have come."

So he went to spread the Good News in the synagogues all over Galilee, and he forced demons out of people.

JESUS CURES A MAN WITH A SKIN DISEASE
(LUKE 5:12–16) ~see also Matthew 8:1–4; Mark 1:40–44~

One day Jesus was in a city where there was a man covered with a serious skin disease. When the man saw Jesus, he bowed with his face to the ground. He begged Jesus, "Sir, if you want to, you can make me clean."

Jesus reached out, touched him, and said, "I want to. So be clean!" Immediately, his skin disease went away.

Jesus ordered him, "Don't tell anyone. Instead, show yourself to the priest. Then offer the sacrifice as Moses commanded as proof to people that you are clean."

The news about Jesus spread even more. Large crowds gathered to hear him and have their diseases cured. But he would go away to places where he could be alone for prayer.

JESUS FORGIVES SINS
(LUKE 5:17–26) ~see also Matthew 9:1–8; Mark 2:1–12~

One day when Jesus was teaching, some Pharisees and experts in Moses' Teachings were present. They had come from every village in Galilee and Judea and from Jerusalem. Jesus had the power of the Lord to heal.

Some men brought a paralyzed man on a stretcher. They tried to take him into the house and put him in front of Jesus. But they could not find a way to get him into the house because of the crowd. So they went up on the roof. They made an opening in the tiles and let the man down on his stretcher among the people. (They lowered him in front of Jesus.)

When Jesus saw their faith, he said, "Sir, your sins are forgiven." The scribes and the Pharisees thought, "Who is this man? He's dishonoring God! Who besides God can forgive sins?"

Jesus knew what they were thinking. So he said to them, "What are you thinking? Is it easier to say, 'Your sins are forgiven,' or to say, 'Get up and walk'? I want you to know that the Son of Man has authority on earth to forgive sins." Then he said to the paralyzed man, "Get up, pick up your stretcher, and go home."

The man immediately stood up in front of them and picked up the stretcher he had been lying on. Praising God, he went home.

Everyone was amazed and praised God. They were filled with awe and said, "We've seen things today we can hardly believe!"

Forgiving Sins

Today more people question the truth of all the miracles performed in the Bible than they do Jesus' ability to forgive sins. Yet, as Jesus asks the crowds in this scene, which is really more significant? The Law and the Prophets, the basic Scriptures upon which people in biblical times based their lives, were clear that sin separated us from God, and it was only through God's intervention and a complex system of sacrifices that sin could be covered up, or atoned for. Although the prophets had spoken of a day when God would usher in a new kingdom and give new hearts perfectly in tune with his own, the existing structures were so deeply ingrained, the people in Jesus' day found it difficult to conceive that complete remission of sin was possible. The man who regained the use of his legs was pleased, but the people went home in awe, wondering perhaps if their sins too might be forgiven one day.

JESUS CHOOSES MATTHEW TO BE A DISCIPLE
(MATTHEW 9:9–13) ~see also Mark 2:13–17; Luke 5:27–32~

When Jesus was leaving that place, he saw a man sitting in a tax office. The man's name was Matthew. Jesus said to him, "Follow me!" So Matthew got up and followed him.

Later Jesus was having dinner at Matthew's house. Many tax collectors and sinners came to eat with Jesus and his disciples. The Pharisees saw this and asked his disciples, "Why does your teacher eat with tax collectors and sinners?"

When Jesus heard that, he said, "Healthy people don't need a doctor; those who are sick do. Learn what this means: 'I want mercy, not sacrifices.' I've come to call sinners, not people who think they have God's approval."

JESUS IS QUESTIONED ABOUT FASTING
(MATTHEW 9:14–17) ~see also Mark 2:18–22; Luke 5:33–39~

Then John's disciples came to Jesus. They said, "Why do we and the Pharisees fast often but your disciples never do?"

Jesus replied, "Can wedding guests be sad while the groom is still with them? The time will come when the groom will be taken away from them. Then they will fast.

"No one patches an old coat with a new piece of cloth that will shrink. When the patch shrinks, it will rip away from the coat, and the tear will become worse. Nor do people pour new wine into old wineskins. If they do, the skins burst, the wine runs out, and the skins are ruined. Rather, people pour new wine into fresh skins, and both are saved."

JESUS RETURNS TO JERUSALEM FOR A FESTIVAL

The growing tension between the Jewish establishment and Jesus starts to come to a head with this visit to Jerusalem. As Jesus continues to perform miraculous healings, he comes into direct confrontation with those most zealous for protecting the Law. These people were so fearful of ever breaking the Law that they had erected a kind of "hedge" around it, comprising all kinds of extra rules and stipulations. Yet, out of a deep desire to avoid offending God, these leaders were in fact driving a wedge between themselves and God. The debate that ensues regarding the lawfulness of healing on the Sabbath contrasts the heavy burden placed on the people by their religious leaders with the life-giving message and ministry of Jesus their Savior.

JESUS CURES A MAN AT THE BETHESDA POOL
(JOHN 5:1–15)

Later, Jesus went to Jerusalem for a Jewish festival.

Near Sheep Gate in Jerusalem was a pool called *Bethesda* in Hebrew. It had five porches. Under these porches a large number of sick people—people who were blind, lame, or paralyzed—used to lie. [*Some manuscripts add*: They would wait for the water to move. People believed that at a certain time an angel from the Lord would go into the pool and stir up the water. The first person who would step into the water after it was stirred up would be cured from whatever disease he had.] One man, who had been sick for 38 years, was lying there. Jesus saw the man lying there and knew that he had been sick for a long time. So Jesus asked the man, "Would you like to get well?"

The sick man answered Jesus, "Sir, I don't have anyone to put me into the pool when the water is stirred. While I'm trying to get there, someone else steps into the pool ahead of me."

Jesus told the man, "Get up, pick up your cot, and walk." The man immediately became well, picked up his cot, and walked.

That happened on a day of worship. So the Jews told the man who had been healed, "This is a day of worship. You're not allowed to carry your cot today."

The man replied, "The man who made me well told me to pick up my cot and walk."

The Jews asked him, "Who is the man who told you to pick it up and walk?" But the man who had been healed didn't know who Jesus was. (Jesus had withdrawn from the crowd.)

Later, Jesus met the man in the temple courtyard and told him, "You're well now. Stop sinning so that something worse doesn't happen to you."

The man went back to the Jews and told them that Jesus was the man who had made him well.

THE SON IS EQUAL TO THE FATHER
(JOHN 5:16–47)

The Jews began to persecute Jesus because he kept healing people on the day of worship. Jesus replied to them, "My Father is working right now, and so am I."

His reply made the Jews more intent on killing him. Not only did he break the laws about the day of worship, but also he made himself equal to God when he said repeatedly that God was his Father.

Jesus said to the Jews, "I can guarantee this truth: The Son cannot do anything on his own. He can do only what he sees the Father doing. Indeed, the Son does exactly what the Father does. The Father loves the Son and shows him everything he is doing. The Father will show him even greater things to do than these things so that you will be amazed. In the same way that the Father brings back the dead and gives them life, the Son gives life to anyone he chooses.

"The Father doesn't judge anyone. He has entrusted judgment entirely to the Son so that everyone will honor the Son as they honor the Father. Whoever doesn't honor the Son doesn't honor the Father who sent him. I can guarantee this truth: Those who listen to what I say and believe in the one who sent me will have eternal life. They won't be judged because they have already passed from death to life.

"I can guarantee this truth: A time is coming (and is now here) when the dead will hear the voice of the Son of God and those who respond to it will live. The Father is the source of life, and he has enabled the Son to be the source of life too.

"He has also given the Son authority to pass judgment because he is the Son of Man. Don't be surprised at what I've just said. A time is coming when all the dead will hear his voice, and they will come out of their tombs. Those who have done good will come back to life and live. But those who have done evil will come back to life and will be judged. I can't do anything on my own. As I listen to the Father, I make my judgments. My judgments are right because I don't try to do what I want but what the one who sent me wants.

"If I testify on my own behalf, what I say isn't true. Someone else testifies on my behalf, and I know that what he says about me is true. You sent people to John the Baptizer, and he testified to the truth. But I don't depend on human testimony. I'm telling you this to save you. John was a lamp that gave off brilliant light. For a time you enjoyed the pleasure of his light. But I have something that testifies more favorably on my behalf than John's testimony. The tasks that the Father gave me to carry out, these tasks which I perform, testify on my behalf. They prove that the Father has sent me. The Father who sent me testifies on my behalf. You have never heard his voice, and you have never seen his form. So you don't have the Father's message within you, because you don't believe in the person he has sent. You study the Scriptures in detail because you think you have the source of eternal life in them. These Scriptures testify on my behalf. Yet, you don't want to come to me to get eternal life.

"I don't accept praise from humans. But I know what kind of people you are. You don't have any love for God. I have come with the authority my Father has given me, but you don't accept me. If someone else comes with his own authority, you will accept him. How can you believe when you accept each other's praise and don't look for the praise that comes from the only God?

"Don't think that I will accuse you in the presence of the Father. Moses, the one you trust, is already accusing you. If you really believed Moses, you would believe me. Moses wrote about me. If you don't believe what Moses wrote, how will you ever believe what I say?"

Father and Son

New Testament scholar Andreas Kostenberger has noted that the Jews at the time of Jesus were not expecting that the Messiah would be able to raise the dead to life (G. K. Beale and D. A. Carson, eds., *Commentary on the New Testament Use of the Old Testament* [Grand Rapids: Baker, 2007], 442). So, Jesus' claim to be able to give life to not just the dead, but also the living, was revolutionary to say the least. In a society committed to monotheism, the claim of co-regency with God was either the grossest kind of blasphemy or the absolute truth. Jesus forced them into a corner and required them to make a decision. There was to be no sitting on the fence. This passage (John 5:16–47), perhaps more than any other, removes any and all possibility of us dismissing Jesus as merely a good moral teacher.

JESUS HAS AUTHORITY OVER THE DAY OF WORSHIP
(MATTHEW 12:1–8) ~see also Mark 2:23–28; Luke 6:1–5~

Then on a day of worship Jesus walked through the grainfields. His disciples were hungry and began to pick the heads of grain to eat.

When the Pharisees saw this, they said to him, "Look! Your disciples are doing something that is not right to do on the day of worship."

Jesus asked them, "Haven't you read what David did when he and his men were hungry? Haven't you read how he went into the house of God and ate the bread of the presence? He and his men had no right to eat those loaves. Only the priests have that right. Or haven't you read in Moses' Teachings that on the day of worship the priests in the temple do things they shouldn't on the day of worship yet remain innocent? I can guarantee that something greater than the temple is here. If you had known what 'I want mercy, not sacrifices' means, you would not have condemned innocent people.

"The Son of Man has authority over the day of worship."

JESUS HEALS ON THE DAY OF WORSHIP
(MATTHEW 12:9–14) ~see also Mark 3:1–6; Luke 6:6–11~

Jesus moved on from there and went into a synagogue. A man with a paralyzed hand was there. The people asked Jesus whether it was right to heal on a day of worship so that they could accuse him of doing something wrong.

Jesus said to them, "Suppose one of you has a sheep. If it falls into a pit on a day of worship, wouldn't you take hold of it and lift it out? Certainly, a human is more valuable than a sheep! So it is right to do good on the day of worship."

Then he said to the man, "Hold out your hand." The man held it out, and it became normal again, as healthy as the other.

The Pharisees left and plotted to kill Jesus. He knew about this, so he left that place.

The Law of the Sabbath

The Sabbath was modeled by God during the creation. "On the seventh day, he stopped the work he had been doing. Then God blessed the seventh day and set it apart as holy, because on that day he stopped all his work of creation" (Gen. 2:2–3). The Sabbath became a vital element in Jewish worship. Included in the Ten Commandments, along with severe penalties for breaking this law, God later rebuked the Israelites for failing to observe the Sabbath and keep it holy. Their failure to keep its observance was part of the reason they were sent into exile. Given their previous experience, the Jews were naturally very careful about what they could and could not do on the Sabbath, and Jesus' actions did not fit into their previously conceived notions about what was and was not acceptable and appropriate. Even though they understood that God did in fact still work on the Sabbath, sustaining his creation, they could not believe that Jesus was God and therefore he was simply guilty of breaking a law that could potentially bring down God's judgment on the entire nation.

JESUS RETURNS TO GALILEE TO PREACH AND HEAL

To talk about "preaching" and "healing" doesn't quite do justice to the enormous impact Jesus had in Galilee. The Sermon on a Mountain contains some of the most profound and significant of his teachings. Offering a completely new perspective on how people should be relating both to God and to each other, the Sermon challenges, provokes, confuses, and amazes all in attendance. Moreover, Jesus doesn't just continue to heal people, he even brings a widow's son back to life. His power over death is one more sign, among many, that he is the Messiah, yet still the majority of people fail to see or understand.

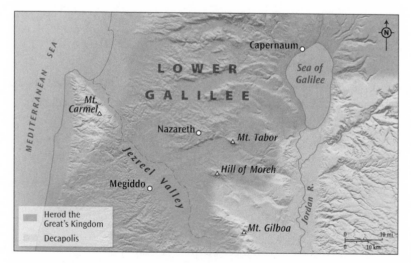

Nazareth/Lower Galilee

MANY PEOPLE ARE CURED
(MARK 3:7–12) ~see also Luke 6:17–19~

Jesus left with his disciples for the Sea of Galilee. A large crowd from Galilee, Judea, Jerusalem, Idumea, and from across the Jordan River, and from around Tyre and Sidon followed him. They came to him because they had heard about everything he was doing. Jesus told his disciples to have a boat ready so that the crowd would not crush him. He had cured so many that everyone with a disease rushed up to him in order to touch him. Whenever people with evil spirits saw him, they would fall down in front of him and shout, "You are the Son of God!" He gave them orders not to tell people who he was.

JESUS APPOINTS TWELVE APOSTLES
(MARK 3:13–19) ~see also Matthew 10:1–4; Luke 6:13–16~

Jesus went up a mountain, called those whom he wanted, and they came to him. He appointed twelve whom he called apostles. They were to accompany him and to be sent out by him to spread the Good News. They also had the authority to force demons out of people.

He appointed these twelve: Simon (whom Jesus named Peter), James and his brother John (Zebedee's sons whom Jesus named Boanerges, which means "Thunderbolts"), Andrew, Philip, Bartholomew, Matthew, Thomas, James (son of Alphaeus), Thaddaeus, Simon the Zealot, and Judas Iscariot (who later betrayed Jesus).

THE SERMON ON A MOUNTAIN: THE BEATITUDES
(MATTHEW 5:1–12)

When Jesus saw the crowds, he went up a mountain and sat down. His disciples came to him, and he began to teach them:

"Blessed are those who recognize they are spiritually helpless.
  The kingdom of heaven belongs to them.
Blessed are those who mourn.
  They will be comforted.
Blessed are those who are gentle.
  They will inherit the earth.
Blessed are those who hunger and thirst for God's approval.
  They will be satisfied.

Blessed are those who show mercy.
They will be treated mercifully.
Blessed are those whose thoughts are pure.
They will see God.
Blessed are those who make peace.
They will be called God's children.
Blessed are those who are persecuted for doing what God approves of.
The kingdom of heaven belongs to them.

"Blessed are you when people insult you,
persecute you,
lie, and say all kinds of evil things about you because of me.
Rejoice and be glad because you have a great reward in heaven!
The prophets who lived before you were persecuted in these ways."

The Old Testament and the Beatitudes

In a world of hungry, hurting, and broken people, the Beatitudes must have struck a deep chord with many of Jesus' listeners. Using language that called to mind promises from the prophets of a new community, a new earth, a new way of living, Jesus aligned himself fully with a way of thinking that stretched back hundreds of years. Craig Blomberg contends that Matthew 5:3–4 possibly alludes to Isaiah 61:1–2, while Matthew 5:6 bears similarities to Isaiah 55:1–3. Key features from several other Beatitudes are reflected in various psalms (Beale and Carson, *Commentary on New Testament Use of the Old Testament,* 20). Significantly, then, Jesus was not simply upending or replacing the Old Testament but saw himself as completely congruent with its message and purpose. The Beatitudes affirm the eternal validity and application of the Old Testament, while reminding us of the vital importance of keeping a God-centered perspective on our priorities in life.

GOD'S PEOPLE MAKE A DIFFERENCE IN THE WORLD
(MATTHEW 5:13–16) ~see also Mark 4:21–23; Luke 11:33~

"You are salt for the earth. But if salt loses its taste, how will it be made salty again? It is no longer good for anything except to be thrown out and trampled on by people.

"You are light for the world. A city cannot be hidden when it is located on a hill. No one lights a lamp and puts it under a basket. Instead, everyone who lights a lamp puts it on a lamp stand. Then its light shines on everyone in the house. In the same way let your light shine in front of people. Then they will see the good that you do and praise your Father in heaven.

JESUS FULFILLS THE OLD TESTAMENT SCRIPTURES
(MATTHEW 5:17–20)

"Don't ever think that I came to set aside Moses' Teachings or the Prophets. I didn't come to set them aside but to make them come true. I can guarantee this truth: Until the earth and the heavens disappear, neither a period nor a comma will disappear from Moses' Teachings before everything has come true. So whoever sets aside any command that seems unimportant and teaches others to do the same will be unimportant in the kingdom of heaven. But whoever does and teaches what the commands say will be called great in the kingdom of heaven. I can guarantee that unless you live a life that has God's approval and do it more faithfully than the scribes and Pharisees, you will never enter the kingdom of heaven."

Jesus Fulfills the Old Testament

A close reading of the Gospels reveals the absolute and primary importance of studying the Old Testament. The authors and principal actors in the New Testament lived and breathed the air of the Old Testament. Many of them had memorized vast portions of the Law and Prophets. Understanding the depth and richness of New Testament teaching can only come about through a thorough and complete understanding of the Old Testament. As Jesus himself said, his life and ministry did not change the fundamental importance of "Moses' Teaching or the Prophets." Rather, he came in order to bring them to completion. What had begun in the Old Testament was now going to be fulfilled, or "made true," in the life, death, and resurrection of Jesus Christ.

JESUS TEACHES ON ANGER, SEXUAL SIN, TAKING OATHS, AND LOVING ENEMIES
(MATTHEW 5:21–48) ~see also Luke 6:27–36~

"You have heard that it was said to your ancestors, 'Never murder. Whoever murders will answer for it in court.' But I can guarantee that whoever is angry with another believer will answer for it in court. Whoever calls another believer an insulting name will answer for it in the highest court. Whoever calls another believer a fool will answer for it in hellfire.

"So if you are offering your gift at the altar and remember there that another believer has something against you, leave your gift at the altar. First go away and make peace with that person. Then come back and offer your gift.

"Make peace quickly with your opponent while you are on the way to court with him. Otherwise, he will hand you over to the judge. Then the judge will hand you over to an officer, who will throw you into prison. I can guarantee this truth: You will never get out until you pay every penny of your fine.

"You have heard that it was said, 'Never commit adultery.' But I can guarantee that whoever looks with lust at a woman has already committed adultery in his heart.

"So if your right eye causes you to sin, tear it out and throw it away. It is better for you to lose a part of your body than to have all of it thrown into hell. And if your right hand leads you to sin, cut it off and throw it away. It is better for you to lose a part of your body than to have all of it go into hell.

"It has also been said, 'Whoever divorces his wife must give her a written notice.' But I can guarantee that any man who divorces his wife for any reason other than unfaithfulness makes her look as though she has committed adultery. Whoever marries a woman divorced in this way makes himself look as though he has committed adultery.

"You have heard that it was said to your ancestors, 'Never break your oath, but give to the Lord what you swore in an oath to give him.' But I tell you don't swear an oath at all. Don't swear an oath by heaven, which is God's throne, or by the earth, which is his footstool, or by Jerusalem, which is the city of the great King. And don't swear an oath by your head. After all, you cannot make one hair black or white. Simply say yes or no. Anything more than that comes from the evil one.

"You have heard that it was said, 'An eye for an eye and a tooth for a tooth.' But I tell you not to oppose an evil person. If someone slaps you on your right cheek, turn your other cheek to him as well. If someone wants to sue you in order to take your shirt, let him have your coat too. If someone forces you to go one mile, go two miles with him. Give to everyone who asks you for something. Don't turn anyone away who wants to borrow something from you.

"You have heard that it was said, 'Love your neighbor, and hate your enemy.' But I tell you this: Love your enemies, and pray for those who persecute you. In this way you show that you are children of your Father in heaven. He makes his sun rise on people whether they are good or evil. He lets rain fall on them whether they are just or unjust. If you love those who love you, do you deserve a reward? Even the tax collectors do that! Are you doing anything remarkable if you welcome only your friends? Everyone does that! That is why you must be perfect as your Father in heaven is perfect."

THE SERMON ON A MOUNTAIN CONTINUES— DON'T DO GOOD WORKS TO BE PRAISED BY PEOPLE
(MATTHEW 6:1–4)

"Be careful not to do your good works in public in order to attract attention. If you do, your Father in heaven will not reward you. So when you give to the poor, don't announce it with trumpet fanfare. This is what hypocrites do in the synagogues and on the streets in order to be praised by people. I can guarantee this truth: That will be their only reward. When you give to the poor, don't let your left hand know what your right hand is doing. Give your contributions privately. Your Father sees what you do in private. He will reward you."

THE LORD'S PRAYER
(MATTHEW 6:5–15) ~see also Luke 11:1–4~

"When you pray, don't be like hypocrites. They like to stand in synagogues and on street corners to pray so that everyone can see them. I can guarantee this truth: That will be their only reward. When you pray, go to your room and close the door. Pray privately to your Father who is with you. Your Father sees what you do in private. He will reward you.

"When you pray, don't ramble like heathens who think they'll be heard if they talk a lot. Don't be like them. Your Father knows what you need before you ask him.

"This is how you should pray:

> Our Father in heaven,
>   let your name be kept holy.
> Let your kingdom come.
>   Let your will be done on earth
>   as it is done in heaven.
> Give us our daily bread today.
> Forgive us as we forgive others.

Don't allow us to be tempted.

Instead, rescue us from the evil one.

"If you forgive the failures of others, your heavenly Father will also forgive you. But if you don't forgive others, your Father will not forgive your failures."

JESUS TEACHES ON FASTING, TRUE RICHES, AND WORRYING
(MATTHEW 6:16–34) ~see also Luke 12:22–34~

"When you fast, stop looking sad like hypocrites. They put on sad faces to make it obvious that they're fasting. I can guarantee this truth: That will be their only reward. When you fast, wash your face and comb your hair. Then your fasting won't be obvious. Instead, it will be obvious to your Father who is with you in private. Your Father sees what you do in private. He will reward you.

"Stop storing up treasures for yourselves on earth, where moths and rust destroy and thieves break in and steal. Instead, store up treasures for yourselves in heaven, where moths and rust don't destroy and thieves don't break in and steal. Your heart will be where your treasure is.

"The eye is the lamp of the body. So if your eye is unclouded, your whole body will be full of light. But if your eye is evil, your whole body will be full of darkness. If the light in you is darkness, how dark it will be!

"No one can serve two masters. He will hate the first master and love the second, or he will be devoted to the first and despise the second. You cannot serve God and wealth.

"So I tell you to stop worrying about what you will eat, drink, or wear. Isn't life more than food and the body more than clothes?

"Look at the birds. They don't plant, harvest, or gather the harvest into barns. Yet, your heavenly Father feeds them. Aren't you worth more than they?

"Can any of you add a single hour to your life by worrying?

"And why worry about clothes? Notice how the flowers grow in the field. They never work or spin yarn for clothes. But I say that not even Solomon in all his majesty was dressed like one of these flowers. That's the way God clothes the grass in the field. Today it's alive, and tomorrow it's thrown into an incinerator. So how much more will he clothe you people who have so little faith?

"Don't ever worry and say, 'What are we going to eat?' or 'What are we going to drink?' or 'What are we going to wear?' Everyone is concerned about these things, and your heavenly Father certainly knows you need all of them. But first, be concerned about his kingdom and what has his approval. Then all these things will be provided for you.

"So don't ever worry about tomorrow. After all, tomorrow will worry about itself. Each day has enough trouble of its own."

THE SERMON ON A MOUNTAIN CONTINUES
(MATTHEW 7:1–29) ~see also Luke 6:31, 37–49; 11:5–13~

"Stop judging so that you will not be judged. Otherwise, you will be judged by the same standard you use to judge others. The standards you use for others will be applied to you. So why do you see the piece of sawdust in another believer's eye and not notice the wooden beam in your own eye? How can you say to another believer, 'Let me take the piece of sawdust out of your eye,' when you have a beam in your own eye? You hypocrite! First remove the beam from your own eye. Then you will see clearly to remove the piece of sawdust from another believer's eye.

"Don't give what is holy to dogs or throw your pearls to pigs. Otherwise, they will trample them and then tear you to pieces.

"Ask, and you will receive. Search, and you will find. Knock, and the door will be opened for you. Everyone who asks will receive. The one who searches will find, and for the one who knocks, the door will be opened.

"If your child asks you for bread, would any of you give him a stone? Or if your child asks for a fish, would you give him a snake? Even though you're evil, you know how to give good gifts to your children. So how much more will your Father in heaven give good things to those who ask him?

"Always do for other people everything you want them to do for you. That is the meaning of Moses' Teachings and the Prophets.

"Enter through the narrow gate because the gate and road that lead to destruction are wide. Many enter through the wide gate. But the narrow gate and the road that lead to life are full of trouble. Only a few people find the narrow gate.

"Beware of false prophets. They come to you disguised as sheep, but in their hearts they are vicious wolves. You will know them by what they produce.

"People don't pick grapes from thornbushes or figs from thistles, do they? In the same way every good tree produces good fruit, but a rotten tree produces bad fruit. A good tree cannot produce bad fruit, and a rotten tree cannot produce good fruit. Any tree that fails to produce good fruit is cut down and thrown into a fire. So you will know them by what they produce.

"Not everyone who says to me, 'Lord, Lord!' will enter the kingdom of heaven, but only the person who does what my Father in heaven wants. Many will say to me on that day, 'Lord, Lord, didn't we prophesy in your name? Didn't we force out demons and do many miracles by the power and authority of your name?' Then I will tell them publicly, 'I've never known you. Get away from me, you evil people.'

"Therefore, everyone who hears what I say and obeys it will be like a wise person who built a house on rock. Rain poured, and floods came. Winds blew and beat against that house. But it did not collapse, because its foundation was on rock.

"Everyone who hears what I say but doesn't obey it will be like a foolish person who built a house on sand. Rain poured, and floods came. Winds blew and struck that house. It collapsed, and the result was a total disaster."

When Jesus finished this speech, the crowds were amazed at his teachings. Unlike their scribes, he taught them with authority.

A BELIEVING ARMY OFFICER
(LUKE 7:1–10) ~see also Matthew 8:5–13~

When Jesus had finished everything he wanted to say to the people, he went to Capernaum. There a Roman army officer's valuable slave was sick and near death. The officer had heard about Jesus and sent some Jewish leaders to him. They were to ask Jesus to come and save the servant's life. They came to Jesus and begged, "He deserves your help. He loves our people and built our synagogue at his own expense."

Jesus went with them. He was not far from the house when the officer sent friends to tell Jesus, "Sir, don't bother. I don't deserve to have you come into my house. That's why I didn't come to you. But just give a command, and let my servant be cured. As you know, I'm in a chain of command and have soldiers at my command. I tell one of them, 'Go!' and he goes, and another, 'Come!' and he comes. I tell my servant, 'Do this!' and he does it."

Jesus was amazed at the officer when he heard these words. He turned to the crowd following him and said, "I can guarantee that I haven't found faith as great as this in Israel."

When the men who had been sent returned to the house, they found the servant healthy again.

JESUS BRINGS A WIDOW'S SON BACK TO LIFE
(LUKE 7:11–17)

Soon afterward, Jesus went to a city called Nain. His disciples and a large crowd went with him. As he came near the entrance to the city, he met a funeral procession. The dead man was a widow's only child. A large crowd from the city was with her.

When the Lord saw her, he felt sorry for her. He said to her, "Don't cry."

He went up to the open coffin, took hold of it, and the men who were carrying it stopped. He said, "Young man, I'm telling you to come back to life!" The dead man sat up and began to talk, and Jesus gave him back to his mother.

Everyone was struck with fear and praised God. They said, "A great prophet has appeared among us," and "God has taken care of his people." This news about Jesus spread throughout Judea and the surrounding region.

Raising the Dead

In a moment that undoubtedly brought to mind a similar miracle performed by Elijah (1 Kings 17:17–24), Jesus brought the widow of Nain's son back to life. As noted previously, only God had the power to raise the dead. Even the Messiah was not expected to be able to perform that kind of miracle. Indeed, it is a miracle that points us back to the original creation narrative, when God created the world out of nothing, simply by speaking; his life-giving words created everything in the universe. Although our understanding of medicine and science has vastly improved over time, even 2,000 years ago everyone knew that death was final. There was no misunderstanding about whether or not the boy was actually dead. The astonishing fact was that Jesus spoke, and the child came back to life.

JESUS SPEAKS ABOUT JOHN
(LUKE 7:18–35) ~see also Matthew 11:2–19~

John's disciples told him about all these things. Then John called two of his disciples and sent them to ask the Lord, "Are you the one who is coming, or should we look for someone else?"

The men came to Jesus and said, "John the Baptizer sent us to ask you, 'Are you the one who is coming, or should we look for someone else?'"

At that time Jesus was curing many people who had diseases, sicknesses, and evil spirits. Also, he was giving back sight to many who were blind.

Jesus answered John's disciples, "Go back, and tell John what you have seen and heard: Blind people see again, lame people are walking, those with skin diseases are made clean, deaf people hear again, dead people are brought back to life, and poor people hear the Good News. Whoever doesn't lose his faith in me is indeed blessed."

When John's messengers had left, Jesus spoke to the crowds about John. "What did you go into the desert to see? Tall grass swaying in the wind? Really, what did you go to see? A man dressed in fine clothes? Those who wear splendid clothes and live in luxury are in royal palaces. Really, what did you go to see? A prophet? Let me tell you that he is far more than a prophet. John is the one about whom Scripture says,

> 'I am sending my messenger ahead of you
>   to prepare the way in front of you.'

I can guarantee that of all the people ever born, no one is greater than John. Yet, the least important person in the kingdom of God is greater than John.

"All the people, including tax collectors, heard John. They admitted that God was right by letting John baptize them. But the Pharisees and the experts in Moses' Teachings rejected God's plan for them. They refused to be baptized.

"How can I describe the people who are living now? What are they like? They are like children who sit in the marketplace and shout to each other,

> 'We played music for you,
>   but you didn't dance.
> We sang a funeral song,
>   but you didn't cry.'

John the Baptizer has come neither eating bread nor drinking wine, and you say, 'There's a demon in him!' The Son of Man has come eating and drinking, and you say, 'Look at him! He's a glutton and a drunk, a friend of tax collectors and sinners!'.

"Yet, wisdom is proved right by all its results."

JESUS WARNS CHORAZIN, BETHSAIDA, AND CAPERNAUM
(MATTHEW 11:20–24)

Then Jesus denounced the cities where he had worked most of his miracles because they had not changed the way they thought and acted. "How horrible it will be for you, Chorazin! How horrible it will be for you, Bethsaida! If the miracles worked in you had been worked in Tyre and Sidon, they would have changed the way they thought and acted long ago in sackcloth and ashes. I can guarantee that judgment day will be better for Tyre and Sidon than for you. And you, Capernaum, will you be lifted to heaven? No, you will go down to hell! If the miracles that had been worked in you had been worked in Sodom, it would still be there today. I can guarantee that judgment day will be better for Sodom than for you."

Rejecting the Truth

This condemnation of the cities of Chorazin, Bethsaida, and Capernaum flies in the face of those who like to conceive of Jesus as a nice moral teacher who wants everyone to get along. Although he taught mercy and love, he also set the bar high for those who had been exposed to the truth and yet rejected it. The primary reason Israel was sent into exile was their failure to love and obey God. Forgetting all that he had done for them in their lives, the people chose instead to worship idols and suffered the dreadful consequences as a result. These three cities were in Galilee, the center of Jesus' ministry, and as such had received the most extensive and sustained exposure to Jesus' miracles and teaching. Yet for the most part the people resisted his call on their lives. While the exile to Babylon, traumatic as it was, had been merely a physical punishment, rejection of Jesus means eternal spiritual punishment. That's simply the way it is, whether for these three cities or for any others who choose to ignore the salvation offered through Jesus Christ.

JESUS PRAISES THE FATHER AND INVITES DISCIPLES TO COME TO HIM
(MATTHEW 11:25–30)

At that time Jesus said, "I praise you, Father, Lord of heaven and earth, for hiding these things from wise and intelligent people and revealing them to little children. Yes, Father, this is what pleased you.

"My Father has turned everything over to me. Only the Father knows the Son. And no one knows the Father except the Son and those to whom the Son is willing to reveal him.

"Come to me, all who are tired from carrying heavy loads, and I will give you rest. Place my yoke over your shoulders, and learn from me, because I am gentle and humble. Then you will find rest for yourselves because my yoke is easy and my burden is light."

A SINFUL WOMAN RECEIVES FORGIVENESS
(LUKE 7:36–50)

One of the Pharisees invited Jesus to eat with him. Jesus went to the Pharisee's house and was eating at the table.

A woman who lived a sinful life in that city found out that Jesus was eating at the Pharisee's house. So she took a bottle of perfume and knelt at his feet. She was crying and washed his feet with her tears. Then she dried his feet with her hair, kissed them over and over again, and poured the perfume on them.

The Pharisee who had invited Jesus saw this and thought, "If this man really were a prophet, he would know what sort of woman is touching him. She's a sinner."

Jesus spoke up, "Simon, I have something to say to you."

Simon replied, "Teacher, you're free to speak."

So Jesus said, "Two men owed a moneylender some money. One owed him five hundred silver coins, and the other owed him fifty. When they couldn't pay it back, he was kind enough to cancel their debts. Now, who do you think will love him the most?"

Simon answered, "I suppose the one who had the largest debt canceled."

Jesus said to him, "You're right!" Then, turning to the woman, he said to Simon, "You see this woman, don't you? I came into your house. You didn't wash my feet. But she has washed my feet with her tears and dried them with her hair. You didn't give me a kiss. But ever since I came in, she has not stopped kissing my feet. You didn't put any olive oil on my head. But she has poured perfume on my feet. That's why I'm telling you that her many sins have been forgiven. Her great love proves that. But whoever receives little forgiveness loves very little."

Then Jesus said to her, "Your sins have been forgiven." The other guests thought, "Who is this man who even forgives sins?"

Jesus said to the woman, "Your faith has saved you. Go in peace!"

WOMEN WHO SUPPORTED JESUS
(LUKE 8:1–3)

After this, Jesus traveled from one city and village to another. He spread the Good News about God's kingdom. The twelve apostles were with him. Also, some women were with him. They had been cured from evil spirits and various illnesses. These women were Mary, also called Magdalene, from whom seven demons had gone out; Joanna, whose husband Chusa was Herod's administrator; Susanna; and many other women. They provided financial support for Jesus and his disciples.

JESUS IS ACCUSED OF WORKING WITH BEELZEBUL
(MATTHEW 12:22–37) ~see also Mark 3:20–30; Luke 11:14–23~

Then some people brought Jesus a man possessed by a demon. The demon made the man blind and unable to talk. Jesus cured him so that he could talk and see.

The crowds were all amazed and said, "Can this man be the Son of David?" When the Pharisees heard this, they said, "This man can force demons out of people only with the help of Beelzebul, the ruler of demons."

Since Jesus knew what they were thinking, he said to them, "Every kingdom divided against itself is ruined. And every city or household divided against itself will not last. If Satan forces Satan out, he is divided against himself. How, then, can his kingdom last? If I force demons out of people with the help of Beelzebul, who helps your followers force them out? That's why they will be your judges. But if I force demons out with the help of God's Spirit, then the kingdom of God has come to you. How can anyone go into a strong man's house and steal his property? First he must tie up the strong man. Then he can go through his house and steal his property.

"Whoever isn't with me is against me. Whoever doesn't gather with me scatters. So I can guarantee that people will be forgiven for any sin or cursing. However, cursing the Spirit will not be forgiven. Whoever speaks a word against the Son of Man will be forgiven. But whoever speaks against the Holy Spirit will not be forgiven in this world or the next.

"Make a tree good, and then its fruit will be good. Or make a tree rotten, and then its fruit will be rotten. A person can recognize a tree by its fruit. You poisonous snakes! How can you evil people say anything good? Your mouth says what comes from inside you. Good people do the good things that are in them. But evil people do the evil things that are in them.

"I can guarantee that on judgment day people will have to give an account of every careless word they say. By your words you will be declared innocent, or by your words you will be declared guilty."

THE SIGN OF JONAH
(MATTHEW 12:38–45) ~see also Luke 11:24–26, 29–32~

Then some scribes and Pharisees said, "Teacher, we want you to show us a miraculous sign."

He responded, "The people of an evil and unfaithful era look for a miraculous sign. But the only sign they will get is the sign of the prophet Jonah. Just as Jonah was in the belly of a huge fish for three days and three nights, so the Son of Man will be in the heart of the earth for three days and three nights. The men of Nineveh will stand up with you at the time of judgment and will condemn you, because they turned to God and changed the way they thought and acted when Jonah spoke his message. But look, someone greater than Jonah is here! The queen from the south will stand up at the time of judgment with you. She will condemn you, because she came from the ends of the earth to hear Solomon's wisdom. But look, someone greater than Solomon is here!

"When an evil spirit comes out of a person, it goes through dry places looking for a place to rest. But it doesn't find any. Then it says, 'I'll go back to the home I left.' When it arrives, it finds the house unoccupied, swept clean, and in order. Then it goes and brings along seven other spirits more evil than itself. They enter and take up permanent residence there. In the end the condition of that person is worse than it was before. That is what will happen to the evil people of this day."

The Sign of Jonah

The story of Jonah was perplexing to many. The Ninevites were a hated and despised people, known for their evil practices and complete rejection of God. Thus, even the idea that God would have sent a prophet to them in the first place was astonishing. That they would have heard his message and actually repented was even more surprising. It is unlikely that any people would have understood that Jesus was talking about his future death and resurrection. There is no evidence that the story of Jonah was interpreted in that way, and they could not have comprehended that this was really the Messiah's plan for salvation. The more shocking allusion from this passage would have been the idea that God was again reaching out to those outside the covenant, that Jesus was planning to bring even Gentiles into the kingdom of God.

THE TRUE FAMILY OF JESUS
(MATTHEW 12:46-50) ~see also Mark 3:31–35; Luke 8:19–21~

While Jesus was still talking to the crowds, his mother and brothers were standing outside. They wanted to talk to him. Someone told him, "Your mother and your brothers are standing outside. They want to talk to you."

He replied to the man speaking to him, "Who is my mother, and who are my brothers?" Pointing with his hand at his disciples, he said, "Look, here are my mother and my brothers. Whoever does what my Father in heaven wants is my brother and sister and mother."

Jesus' True Family

Jesus, who respected his mother's promptings at the wedding in Cana, was clearly not speaking in a derogatory manner about his parents. It would make no sense for Jesus to break God's commandment to honor his mother and father. So what did Jesus mean? In the middle of a rapidly growing ministry, as he seeks to expand the people's understanding of who he really is, Jesus is instead pointing to the centrality of God's will in their living lives of obedience to him. Jesus is not concerned with just healing and preaching, he is gathering people to himself, committed followers whom he can depend upon to take the gospel to the world after his departure. He knows that time is short, and thus it was of critical importance for the disciples to understand the primary importance of obedience to the plans of "my Father in heaven."

JESUS TEACHES ABOUT GOD'S KINGDOM

As the crowds grew in size and Jesus' popularity increased, true under-standing of the message he preached dropped dramatically. The parables were in some ways intended to separate those who were truly seeking God from the mere hangers-on. They were messages intended for an audience who was paying close attention, seeking to understand what this man of God was really saying. For those few people, these simple stories utilizing themes and images from everyday life became powerful metaphors about the dawning of God's kingdom.

A STORY ABOUT A FARMER
(MARK 4:1–20) ~see also Matthew 13:1–23; Luke 8:4–15~

Jesus began to teach again by the Sea of Galilee. A very large crowd gathered around him, so he got into a boat and sat in it. The boat was in the water while the entire crowd lined the shore. He used stories as illustrations to teach them many things.

While he was teaching them, he said, "Listen! A farmer went to plant seed. Some seeds were planted along the road, and birds came and devoured them. Other seeds were planted on rocky ground, where there wasn't much soil. The plants sprouted quickly because the soil wasn't deep. When the sun came up, they were scorched. They didn't have any roots, so they withered. Other seeds were planted among thornbushes. The thornbushes grew up and choked them, and they didn't produce anything. But other seeds were planted on good ground, sprouted, and produced thirty, sixty, or one hundred times as much as was planted." He added, "Let the person who has ears listen!"

When he was alone with his followers and the twelve apostles, they asked him about the stories.

Jesus replied to them, "The mystery about the kingdom of God has been given directly to you. To those on the outside, it is given in stories:

'They see clearly but don't perceive.
They hear clearly but don't understand.
They never return to me
and are never forgiven.'"

Jesus asked them, "Don't you understand this story? How, then, will you understand any of the stories I use as illustrations?

"The farmer plants the word. Some people are like seeds that were planted along the road. Whenever they hear the word, Satan comes at once and takes away the word that was planted in them. Other people are like seeds that were planted on rocky ground. Whenever they hear the word, they accept it at once with joy. But they don't develop any roots. They last for a short time. When suffering or persecution comes along because of the word, they immediately fall from faith. Other people are like seeds planted among thornbushes. They hear the word, but the worries of life, the deceitful pleasures of riches, and the desires for other things take over. They choke the word so that it can't produce anything. Others are like seeds planted on good ground. They hear the word, accept it, and produce crops—thirty, sixty, or one hundred times as much as was planted."

God's Kingdom

Jesus used all kinds of analogies and illustrations to help the people understand. He used the example of a farmer sowing seed, explaining that the kingdom of God will grow and expand, and as participants we are to bear fruit. He said the kingdom is like a bright light shining in the darkness, guiding the way. Therefore it is not to be hidden, but revealed to all. He also said the kingdom is like a field where weeds and wheat grow together, only to be separated during the harvest, an allusion to the fact that both the righteous and unrighteous will live together until the time of judgment. In every example it is clear that God's kingdom and God's values are radically opposed to the kingdom and values of this world, with its focus on self-satisfaction and self-absorption. The kingdom will grow despite the impact of sin and any attempts of Satan, and will unequivocally triumph in the end.

A STORY ABOUT A LAMP
(MARK 4:21–25)

Jesus said to them, "Does anyone bring a lamp into a room to put it under a basket or under a bed? Isn't it put on a lamp stand? There is nothing hidden that will not be revealed. There is nothing kept secret that will not come to light. Let the person who has ears listen!"

He went on to say, "Pay attention to what you're listening to! Knowledge will be measured out to you by the measure of attention you give. This is the way knowledge increases. Those who understand these mysteries will be given more knowledge. However, some people don't understand these mysteries. Even what they understand will be taken away from them."

A STORY ABOUT SEEDS THAT GROW
(MARK 4:26–29)

Jesus said, "The kingdom of God is like a man who scatters seeds on the ground. He sleeps at night and is awake during the day. The seeds sprout and grow, although the man doesn't know how. The ground produces grain by itself. First the green blade appears, then the head, then the head full of grain. As soon as the grain is ready, he cuts it with a sickle, because harvest time has come."

STORIES ABOUT WEEDS, SEEDS, YEAST, AND WHEAT
(MATTHEW 13:24–43) ~see also Mark 4:30–34; Luke 13:18–21~

Jesus used another illustration. He said, "The kingdom of heaven is like a man who planted good seed in his field. But while people were asleep, his enemy planted weeds in the wheat field and went away. When the wheat came up and formed kernels, weeds appeared.

"The owner's workers came to him and asked, 'Sir, didn't you plant good seed in your field? Where did the weeds come from?'

"He told them, 'An enemy did this.'

"His workers asked him, 'Do you want us to pull out the weeds?'

"He replied, 'No. If you pull out the weeds, you may pull out the wheat with them. Let both grow together until the harvest. When the grain is cut, I will tell the workers to gather the weeds first and tie them in bundles to be burned. But I'll have them bring the wheat into my barn.'"

Jesus used another illustration. He said, "The kingdom of heaven is like a mustard seed that someone planted in a field. It's one of the smallest seeds. However, when it has grown, it is taller than the garden plants. It becomes a tree that is large enough for birds to nest in its branches."

He used another illustration. "The kingdom of heaven is like yeast that a woman mixed into a large amount of flour until the yeast worked its way through all the dough."

Jesus used illustrations to tell the crowds all these things. He did not tell them anything without illustrating it with a story. So what the prophet had said came true:

"I will open my mouth to illustrate points.
I will tell what has been hidden since the world was made."

When Jesus had sent the people away, he went into the house. His disciples came to him and said, "Explain what the illustration of the weeds in the field means."

He answered, "The one who plants the good seeds is the Son of Man. The field is the world. The good seeds are those who belong to the kingdom. The weeds are those who belong to the evil one. The enemy who planted them is the devil. The harvest is the end of the world. The workers are angels. Just as weeds are gathered and burned, so it will be at the end of time. The Son of Man will send his angels. They will gather everything in his kingdom that causes people to sin and everyone who does evil. The angels will throw them into a blazing furnace. People will cry and be in extreme pain there. Then the people who have God's approval will shine like the sun in their Father's kingdom. Let the person who has ears listen!"

STORIES ABOUT A TREASURE, A MERCHANT, AND A NET
(MATTHEW 13:44–53)

"The kingdom of heaven is like a treasure buried in a field. When a man discovered it, he buried it again. He was so delighted with it that he went away, sold everything he had, and bought that field.

"Also, the kingdom of heaven is like a merchant who was searching for fine pearls. When he found a valuable pearl, he went away, sold everything he had, and bought it.

"Also, the kingdom of heaven is like a net that was thrown into the sea. It gathered all kinds of fish. When it was full, they pulled it to the shore. Then they sat down, gathered the good fish into containers, and threw the bad ones away. The same thing will happen at the end of time. The angels will go out and separate the evil people from people who have God's approval. Then the angels will throw the evil people into a blazing furnace. They will cry and be in extreme pain there.

"Have you understood all of this?"

"Yes," they answered.

So Jesus said to them, "That is why every scribe who has become a disciple of the kingdom of heaven is like a home owner. He brings new and old things out of his treasure chest."

When Jesus had finished these illustrations, he left that place.

JESUS CROSSES THE SEA OF GALILEE

We live in a culture obsessed with power. Since our lives are relatively short and quite unpredictable, we tend to look for areas in which we can control our circumstances. Some of us use money in an effort to exert power and control over our physical and emotional lives. Others use brute force to steal power and enforce it for themselves. Jesus came to overturn these petty human attempts at controlling life. Certainly, as many would attest, Jesus lived and preached an ethic of love and mercy that subverted selfishness and pride. Yet at crucial moments in his ministry Jesus also exercised his divine power in some spectacular ways, such as calming the storm and curing the demon-possessed man.

JESUS CALMS THE SEA
(LUKE 8:22–25) *~see also Matthew 8:23–27; Mark 4:35–41~*

One day Jesus and his disciples got into a boat. He said to them, "Let's cross to the other side of the lake." So they started out. As they were sailing along, Jesus fell asleep.

A violent storm came across the lake. The boat was taking on water, and they were in danger. They went to him, woke him up, and said, "Master! Master! We're going to die!"

Then he got up and ordered the wind and the waves to stop. The wind stopped, and the sea became calm. He asked them, "Where is your faith?"

Frightened and amazed, they asked each other, "Who is this man? He gives orders to the wind and the water, and they obey him!"

Absolute Power

Imagine telling the rain to stop, the sun to shine, the wind to cease—and nature obeys. Jesus did just that. With a word he gave orders to the wind and the water, and they obeyed him. As God spoke the world into existence, creating the land and the sea with just his words, so Jesus also demonstrated complete control over the physical creation. Whereas even some charlatans and "doctors" might have on occasion been able to heal people, nobody had ever, ever, been able to control the weather. The physical world had always been the sole domain of the gods. Thus, with this miracle Jesus provided the disciples with a clear demonstration of his absolute divinity.

JESUS CURES A DEMON-POSSESSED MAN
(LUKE 8:26–39) ~see also Matthew 8:28–34; Mark 5:1–20~

They landed in the region of the Gerasenes across from Galilee. When Jesus stepped out on the shore, a certain man from the city met him. The man was possessed by demons and had not worn clothes for a long time. He would not stay in a house but lived in the tombs. When he saw Jesus, he shouted, fell in front of him, and said in a loud voice, "Why are you bothering me, Jesus, Son of the Most High God? I beg you not to torture me!" Jesus ordered the evil spirit to come out of the man. (The evil spirit had controlled the man for a long time. People had kept him under guard. He was chained hand and foot. But he would break the chains. Then the demon would force him to go into the desert.)

Jesus asked him, "What is your name?"

He answered, "Legion [Six Thousand]." (Many demons had entered him.) The demons begged Jesus not to order them to go into the bottomless pit.

A large herd of pigs was feeding on a mountainside. The demons begged Jesus to let them enter those pigs. So he let them do this. The demons came out of the man and went into the pigs. Then the herd rushed down the cliff into the lake and drowned.

When those who had taken care of the pigs saw what had happened, they ran away. They reported everything in the city and countryside. The people went to see what had happened. They came to Jesus and found the man from whom the demons had gone out. Dressed and in his right mind, he was sitting at Jesus' feet. The people were frightened. Those who had seen this told the people how Jesus had restored the demon-possessed man to health.

Then all the people from the surrounding region of the Gerasenes asked Jesus to leave because they were terrified.

Jesus got into a boat and started back. The man from whom the demons had gone out begged him, "Let me go with you."

But Jesus sent the man away and told him, "Go home to your family, and tell them how much God has done for you." So the man left. He went through the whole city and told people how much Jesus had done for him.

Power over Evil

Many people believe that the Bible teaches that the powers of good and evil are equal, opposite forces locked in a battle that could go either way. There were many religious philosophies of this sort among the Greeks, yet the Bible clearly teaches a different message. According to the Old Testament, there is one God, who made everything. All other entities, without exception, fall under his jurisdiction. Satan is not co-equal with God; he exists under God. The New Testament maintains that same emphasis, running contrary to prevailing patterns of thought at the time, teaching that there is still only one God, and he alone is sovereign over all creatures, whether physical or spiritual. Although the dramatic healing of this man benefited him personally, it also shows God's total control and power over everything in the universe, including demons.

JESUS RETURNS TO GALILEE

On his return to Galilee, we see a noticeable change in Jesus' ministry. Whereas before there were times when he was more circumspect in his language, Jesus moves now to a more direct form of address, openly challenging both common people as well as the religious leaders. He does not avoid conflict but sometimes even seems to seek it out, provoking, challenging, stimulating the people to rethink their understanding of the Scriptures. It is as if Jesus can sense that his time is short, and the burden he carries is getting heavier and heavier. There is a new urgency in his voice as he looks for God's hand to be at work transforming hearts and drawing them to himself.

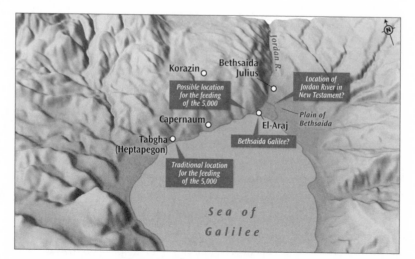

The Feeding of the Five Thousand

A SYNAGOGUE LEADER'S DAUGHTER AND THE WOMAN WITH CHRONIC BLEEDING
(MATTHEW 9:18–26) ~see also Mark 5:21–43; Luke 8:40–56~

A synagogue leader came to Jesus while he was talking to John's disciples. He bowed down in front of Jesus and said, "My daughter just died. Come, lay your hand on her, and she will live."

Jesus and his disciples got up and followed the man.

Then a woman came up behind Jesus and touched the edge of his clothes. She had been suffering from chronic bleeding for twelve years. She thought, "If I only touch his clothes, I'll get well."

When Jesus turned and saw her he said, "Cheer up, daughter! Your faith has made you well." At that very moment the woman became well.

Jesus came to the synagogue leader's house. He saw flute players and a noisy crowd. He said to them, "Leave! The girl is not dead. She's sleeping." But they laughed at him.

When the crowd had been put outside, Jesus went in, took her hand, and the girl came back to life.

The news about this spread throughout that region.

JESUS HEALS, CASTS OUT DEMONS, AND SHOWS COMPASSION TO ALL
(MATTHEW 9:27–38)

When Jesus left that place, two blind men followed him. They shouted, "Have mercy on us, Son of David."

Jesus went into a house, and the blind men followed him. He said to them, "Do you believe that I can do this?"

"Yes, Lord," they answered.

He touched their eyes and said, "What you have believed will be done for you!" Then they could see.

He warned them, "Don't let anyone know about this!" But they went out and spread the news about him throughout that region.

As they were leaving, some people brought a man to Jesus. The man was unable to talk because he was possessed by a demon. But as soon as the demon was forced out, the man began to speak.

The crowds were amazed and said, "We have never seen anything like this in Israel!"

But the Pharisees said, "He forces demons out of people with the help of the ruler of demons."

Jesus went to all the towns and villages. He taught in the synagogues and spread the Good News of the kingdom. He also cured every disease and sickness.

When he saw the crowds, he felt sorry for them. They were troubled and helpless like sheep without a shepherd. Then he said to his disciples, "The harvest is large, but the workers are few. So ask the Lord who gives this harvest to send workers to harvest his crops."

NAZARETH REJECTS JESUS
(MARK 6:1–6) ~see also Matthew 13:54–58; Luke 4:14–30~

Jesus left that place and went to his hometown. His disciples followed him. When the day of worship came, he began to teach in the synagogue. He amazed many who heard him. They asked, "Where did this man get these ideas? Who gave him this kind of wisdom and the ability to do such great miracles? Isn't this the carpenter, the son of Mary, and the brother of James, Joseph, Judas, and Simon? Aren't his sisters here with us?" So they took offense at him.

But Jesus told them, "The only place a prophet isn't honored is in his hometown, among his relatives, and in his own house." He couldn't work any miracles there except to lay his hands on a few sick people and cure them. Their unbelief amazed him.

Then Jesus went around to the villages and taught.

JESUS SENDS OUT THE TWELVE
(MATTHEW 10:5–11:1) ~see also Mark 6:7–13; Luke 9:1–6~

Jesus sent these twelve out with the following instructions: "Don't go among people who are not Jewish or into any Samaritan city. Instead, go to the lost sheep of the nation of Israel. As you go, spread this message: 'The kingdom of heaven is near.' Cure the sick, bring the dead back to life, cleanse those with skin diseases, and force demons out of people. Give these things without charging, since you received them without paying.

"Don't take any gold, silver, or even copper coins in your pockets. Don't take a traveling bag for the trip, a change of clothes, sandals, or a walking stick. After all, the worker deserves to have his needs met.

"When you go into a city or village, look for people who will listen to you there. Stay with them until you leave that place. When you go into a house, greet the family. If it is a family that listens to you, allow your greeting to stand. But if it is not receptive, take back your greeting. If anyone doesn't welcome you or listen to what you say, leave that house or city, and shake its dust off your feet. I can guarantee this truth: Judgment day will be better for Sodom and Gomorrah than for that city.

"I'm sending you out like sheep among wolves. So be as cunning as snakes but as innocent as doves. Watch out for people who will hand you over to the Jewish courts and whip you in their synagogues. Because of me you will even be brought in front of governors and kings to testify to them and to everyone in the world. When they hand you over to the authorities, don't worry about what to say or how to say it. When the time comes, you will be given what to say. Indeed, you're not the ones who will be speaking. The Spirit of your Father will be speaking through you.

"Brother will hand over brother to death; a father will hand over his child. Children will rebel against their parents and kill them. Everyone will hate you because you are committed to me. But the person who patiently endures to the end will be saved. So when they persecute you in one city, flee to another. I can guarantee this truth: Before you have gone through every city in Israel, the Son of Man will come.

"A student is not better than his teacher. Nor is a slave better than his owner. It is enough for a student to become like his teacher and a slave like his owner. If they have called the owner of the house Beelzebul, they will certainly call the family members the same name. So don't be afraid of them. Nothing has been covered that will not be exposed. Whatever is secret will be made known. Tell in the daylight what I say to you in the dark. Shout from the housetops what you hear whispered. Don't be afraid of those who kill the body but cannot kill the soul. Instead, fear the one who can destroy both body and soul in hell.

"Aren't two sparrows sold for a penny? Not one of them will fall to the ground without your Father's permission. Every hair on your head has been counted. Don't be afraid! You are worth more than many sparrows.

"So I will acknowledge in front of my Father in heaven that person who acknowledges me in front of others. But I will tell my Father in heaven that I don't know the person who tells others that he doesn't know me.

"Don't think that I came to bring peace to earth. I didn't come to bring peace but conflict. I came to turn a man against his father, a daughter against her mother, a daughter-in-law against her mother-in-law. A person's enemies will be the members of his own family.

"The person who loves his father or mother more than me does not deserve to be my disciple. The person who loves a son or daughter more than me does not deserve to be my disciple. Whoever doesn't take up his cross and follow me doesn't deserve to be my disciple. The person who tries to preserve his life will lose it, but the person who loses his life for me will preserve it.

"The person who welcomes you welcomes me, and the person who welcomes me welcomes the one who sent me. The person who welcomes a prophet as a prophet will receive a prophet's reward. The person who welcomes a righteous person as a righteous person will receive a righteous person's reward. I can guarantee this truth: Whoever gives any of my humble followers a cup of cold water because that person is my disciple will certainly never lose his reward."

After Jesus finished giving his twelve disciples these instructions, he moved on from there to teach his message in their cities.

HEROD KILLS JOHN THE BAPTIST
(MATTHEW 14:1–12) ~see also Mark 6:14–29; Luke 9:7–9~

At that time Herod, ruler of Galilee, heard the news about Jesus. He said to his officials, "This is John the Baptizer! He has come back to life. That's why he has the power to perform these miracles."

Herod had arrested John, tied him up, and put him in prison. Herod did this for Herodias, the wife of his brother Philip. John had been telling Herod, "It's not right for you to be married to her." So Herod wanted to kill John. However, he was afraid of the people because they thought John was a prophet.

When Herod celebrated his birthday, Herodias' daughter danced for his guests. Herod was so delighted with her that he swore he would give her anything she wanted.

Urged by her mother, she said, "Give me the head of John the Baptizer on a platter."

The king regretted his promise. But because of his oath and his guests, he ordered that her wish be granted. He had John's head cut off in prison. So the head was brought on a platter and given to the girl, who took it to her mother.

John's disciples came for the body and buried it. Then they went to tell Jesus.

JESUS FEEDS MORE THAN FIVE THOUSAND
(JOHN 6:1–15) ~see also Matthew 14:13–21; Mark 6:30–44; Luke 9:10–17~

Jesus later crossed to the other side of the Sea of Galilee (or the Sea of Tiberias). A large crowd followed him because they saw the miracles that he performed for the sick. Jesus went up a mountain and sat with his disciples. The time for the Jewish Passover festival was near.

As Jesus saw a large crowd coming to him, he said to Philip, "Where can we buy bread for these people to eat?" Jesus asked this question to test him but he already knew what to do.

Philip answered, "We would need about a year's wages to buy enough bread for each of them to have a piece."

One of Jesus' disciples, Andrew, who was Simon Peter's brother, told him, "A boy who has five loaves of barley bread and two small fish is here. But they won't go very far for so many people."

Jesus said, "Have the people sit down."

The people had plenty of grass to sit on. (There were about 5,000 men in the crowd.)

Jesus took the loaves, gave thanks, and distributed them to the people who were sitting there. He did the same thing with the fish. All the people ate as much as they wanted.

When the people were full, Jesus told his disciples, "Gather the leftover pieces so that nothing will be wasted." The disciples gathered the leftover pieces of bread and filled twelve baskets.

When the people saw the miracle Jesus performed, they said, "This man is certainly the prophet who is to come into the world." Jesus realized that the people intended to take him by force and make him king. So he returned to the mountain by himself.

JESUS WALKS ON THE SEA
(JOHN 6:16–21) ~see also Matthew 14:22–33; Mark 6:45–52~

When evening came, his disciples went to the sea. They got into a boat and started to cross the sea to the city of Capernaum. By this time it was dark, and Jesus had not yet come to them. A strong wind started to blow and stir up the sea.

After they had rowed three or four miles, they saw Jesus walking on the sea. He was coming near the boat, and they became terrified.

Jesus told them, "It's me. Don't be afraid!"

So they were willing to help Jesus into the boat. Immediately, the boat reached the shore where they were going.

JESUS HEALS MANY
(MARK 6:53–56) ~see also Matthew 14:34–36~

They crossed the sea, came to shore at Gennesaret, and anchored there.

As soon as they stepped out of the boat, the people recognized Jesus. They ran all over the countryside and began to carry the sick on cots to any place where they heard he was. Whenever he would go into villages, cities, or farms, people would put their sick in the marketplaces. They begged him to let them touch the edge of his clothes. Everyone who touched his clothes was made well.

JESUS IS THE BREAD OF LIFE
(JOHN 6:22–71)

On the next day the people were still on the other side of the sea. They noticed that only one boat was there and that Jesus had not stepped into that boat with his disciples. The disciples had gone away without him. Other boats from Tiberias arrived near the place where they had eaten the bread after the Lord gave thanks. When the people saw that neither Jesus nor his disciples were there, they got into these boats and went to the city of Capernaum to look for Jesus. When they found him on the other side of the sea, they asked him, "Rabbi, when did you get here?"

Jesus replied to them, "I can guarantee this truth: You're not looking for me because you saw miracles. You are looking for me because you ate as much of those loaves as you wanted. Don't work for food that spoils. Instead, work for the food that lasts into eternal life. This is the food the Son of Man will give you. After all, the Father has placed his seal of approval on him."

The people asked Jesus, "What does God want us to do?"

Jesus replied to them, "God wants to do something for you so that you believe in the one whom he has sent."

The people asked him, "What miracle are you going to perform so that we can see it and believe in you? What are you going to do? Our ancestors ate the manna in the desert. Scripture says, 'He gave them bread from heaven to eat.'"

Jesus said to them, "I can guarantee this truth: Moses didn't give you bread from heaven, but my Father gives you the true bread from heaven. God's bread is the man who comes from heaven and gives life to the world."

They said to him, "Sir, give us this bread all the time."

Jesus told them, "I am the bread of life. Whoever comes to me will never become hungry, and whoever believes in me will never become thirsty. I've told you that you have seen me. However, you don't believe in me. Everyone whom the Father gives me will come to me. I will never turn away anyone who comes to me. I haven't come from heaven to do what I want to do. I've come to do what the one who sent me wants me to do. The one who sent me doesn't want me to lose any of those he gave me. He wants me to bring them back to life on the last day. My Father wants all those who see the Son and believe in him to have eternal life. He wants me to bring them back to life on the last day."

The Jews began to criticize Jesus for saying, "I am the bread that came from heaven." They asked, "Isn't this man Jesus, Joseph's son? Don't we know his father and mother? How can he say now, 'I came from heaven'?"

Jesus responded, "Stop criticizing me! People cannot come to me unless the Father who sent me brings them to me. I will bring these people back to life on the last day. The prophets wrote, 'God will teach everyone.' Those who do what they have learned from the Father come to me. I'm saying that no one has seen the Father. Only the one who is from God has seen the Father. I can guarantee this truth: Every believer has eternal life.

"I am the bread of life. Your ancestors ate the manna in the desert and died. This is the bread that comes from heaven so that whoever eats it won't die. I am the living bread that came from heaven. Whoever eats this bread will live forever. The bread I will give to bring life to the world is my flesh."

The Jews began to quarrel with each other. They said, "How can this man give us his flesh to eat?"

Jesus told them, "I can guarantee this truth: If you don't eat the flesh of the Son of Man and drink his blood, you don't have the source of life in you. Those who eat my flesh and drink my blood have eternal life, and I will bring them back to life on the last day. My flesh is true food, and my blood is true drink. Those who eat my flesh and drink my blood live in me, and I live in them. The Father who has life sent me, and I live because of the Father. So those who feed on me will live because of me. This is the bread that came from heaven. It is not like the bread your ancestors ate. They eventually died. Those who eat this bread will live forever."

Jesus said this while he was teaching in a synagogue in Capernaum. When many of Jesus' disciples heard him, they said, "What he says is hard to accept. Who wants to listen to him anymore?"

Jesus was aware that his disciples were criticizing his message. So Jesus asked them, "Did what I say make you lose faith? What if you see the Son of Man go where he was before? Life is spiritual. Your physical existence doesn't contribute to that life. The words that I have spoken to you are spiritual. They are life. But some of you don't believe." Jesus knew from the beginning those who wouldn't believe and the one who would betray him. So he added, "That is why I told you that people cannot come to me unless the Father provides the way."

Jesus' speech made many of his disciples go back to the lives they had led before they followed Jesus. So Jesus asked the twelve apostles, "Do you want to leave me too?"

Simon Peter answered Jesus, "Lord, to what person could we go? Your words give eternal life. Besides, we believe and know that you are the Holy One of God."

Jesus replied, "I chose all twelve of you. Yet, one of you is a devil." Jesus meant Judas, son of Simon Iscariot. Judas, who was one of the twelve apostles, would later betray Jesus.

JESUS CHALLENGES THE PHARISEES' TRADITIONS
(MARK 7:1–23) ~see also Matthew 15:1–20~

The Pharisees and some scribes who had come from Jerusalem gathered around Jesus. They saw that some of his disciples were unclean because they ate without washing their hands.

(The Pharisees, like all other Jewish people, don't eat unless they have properly washed their hands. They follow the traditions of their ancestors. When they come from the marketplace, they don't eat unless they have washed first. They have been taught to follow many other rules. For example, they must also wash their cups, jars, brass pots, and dinner tables.)

The Pharisees and the scribes asked Jesus, "Why don't your disciples follow the traditions taught by our ancestors? They are unclean because they don't wash their hands before they eat!"

Jesus told them, "Isaiah was right when he prophesied about you hypocrites in Scripture:

'These people honor me with their lips,
    but their hearts are far from me.
Their worship of me is pointless,
    because their teachings are rules made by humans.'

"You abandon the commandments of God to follow human traditions." He added, "You have no trouble rejecting the commandments of God in order to keep your own traditions! For example, Moses said, 'Honor your father and your mother' and 'Whoever curses father or mother must be put to death.' But you say, 'If a person tells his father or mother that whatever he might have used to help them is *corban* (that is, an offering to God), he no longer has to do anything for his father or mother.' Because of your traditions you have destroyed the authority of God's word. And you do many other things like that."

Then he called the crowd again and said to them, "Listen to me, all of you, and try to understand! Nothing that goes into a person from the outside can make him unclean. It's what comes out of a person that makes him unclean. Let the person who has ears listen!"

When he had left the people and gone home, his disciples asked him about this illustration.

Jesus said to them, "Don't you understand? Don't you know that whatever goes into a person from the outside can't make him unclean? It doesn't go into his thoughts but into his stomach and then into a toilet." (By saying this, Jesus declared all foods acceptable.) He continued, "It's what comes out of a person that makes him unclean. Evil thoughts, sexual sins, stealing, murder, adultery, greed, wickedness, cheating, shameless lust, envy, cursing, arrogance, and foolishness come from within a person. All these evils come from within and make a person unclean."

Jesus and the Pharisees

Although we have come to think of the word *Pharisee* as entirely negative, not every Pharisee was bad. Indeed, the Pharisees had initially seen themselves as a reform movement motivated by an honest zeal for the Lord. Given the large number of references to them in the Gospels, it is clear that they played an important role in the lives of the Jewish people at the time of Jesus. It was perhaps their very zeal for the Law that caused such friction with Jesus. Jesus, after all, was not just another man, but God. The Law was his law. Tension arose on two fronts. The first was their steadfast refusal to listen to Jesus. The second was their failure to uphold the very Law that they claimed to hold so dear. In many instances, as Jesus was always quick to point out, their desire to protect the Law actually pushed them farther away from God. In their radical obsession with rules, they lost sight of their relationship with him. When Jesus pointed this out, they could only respond with anger.

JESUS TRAVELS TO TYRE AND SIDON

One of the foundational elements of the Jewish faith was God's promise to Abraham, "I will make you a great nation, I will bless you. I will make your name great, and you will be a blessing. I will bless those who bless you, and

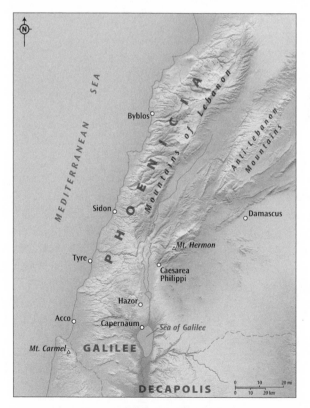

Tyre and Sidon in Phoenicia

whoever curses you, I will curse. Through you every family on earth will be blessed" (Gen. 12:2–3). Although the bulk of Jesus' ministry, especially as recorded by Matthew, was directed toward the people of Israel, surely the Abrahamic covenant was in mind here as Jesus intentionally went to a Gentile region to preach and heal.

THE FAITH OF A CANAANITE WOMAN
(MATTHEW 15:21–28) ~see also Mark 7:24–30~

Jesus left that place and went to the region of Tyre and Sidon.

A Canaanite woman from that territory came to him and began to shout, "Have mercy on me, Lord, Son of David! My daughter is tormented by a demon."

But he did not answer her at all. Then his disciples came to him and urged him, "Send her away. She keeps shouting behind us."

Jesus responded, "I was sent only to the lost sheep of the nation of Israel."

She came to him, bowed down, and said, "Lord, help me!"

Jesus replied, "It's not right to take the children's food and throw it to the dogs."

She said, "You're right, Lord. But even the dogs eat scraps that fall from their masters' tables."

Then Jesus answered her, "Woman, you have strong faith! What you wanted will be done for you." At that moment her daughter was cured.

Going into Gentile Territory

For a chosen people, a nation set apart from all others as God's special possession, the Jews were for the most part quite careful about intermingling with Gentiles. Yet, Jesus was about to usher in a new kingdom, a new period in history that would see the "grafting in" of other peoples into the great and noble family tree of Abraham. Moments such as this visit to the region of Tyre and Sidon prefigure the later incredible missionary work of Paul, who preached the Good News to the Gentiles. Not only does Jesus go into Gentile territory, not only does he heal this woman's daughter, he also commends the woman for her faith in the process. Although Jesus' primary mission was initially to the Jews, people in that day would have found it shocking to consider that perhaps the effects of his ministry would expand widely enough to include the Gentiles as well.

JESUS TEACHES AROUND THE SEA OF GALILEE

People everywhere clamored for signs. However, not everyone was necessarily seeking more illumination. Some came simply for the show. Others challenged Jesus in order to be confrontational. Yet, still others had very real, deep needs, and sought Jesus out for healing and help. When they confessed their need, Jesus responded. Note that while Jesus showed little patience for the religious leaders and their stubborn disbelief, he was amazingly patient with the disciples as they wrestled with their confusion and doubt.

JESUS CURES MANY PEOPLE
(MATTHEW 15:29–31)

Jesus moved on from there and went along the Sea of Galilee. Then he went up a mountain and sat there.

A large crowd came to him, bringing with them the lame, blind, disabled, those unable to talk, and many others. They laid them at his feet, and he cured them. The crowd was amazed to see mute people talking, the disabled cured, the lame walking, and the blind seeing. So they praised the God of Israel.

JESUS FEEDS FOUR THOUSAND
(MARK 8:1–10) ~*see also Matthew 15:32–39*~

About that time there was once again a large crowd with nothing to eat. Jesus called his disciples and said to them, "I feel sorry for the people. They have been with me three days now and have nothing to eat. If I send them home before they've eaten, they will become exhausted on the road. Some of them have come a long distance."

His disciples asked him, "Where could anyone get enough bread to feed these people in this place where no one lives?"

Jesus asked them, "How many loaves of bread do you have?"

They answered, "Seven."

He ordered the crowd to sit down on the ground. He took the seven loaves and gave thanks to God. Then he broke the bread and gave it to his disciples to serve to the people. They also had a few small fish. He blessed them and said that the fish should also be served to the people. The people ate as much as they wanted. The disciples picked up the leftover pieces and filled seven large baskets. About four thousand people were there. Then he sent the people on their way.

After that, Jesus and his disciples got into a boat and went into the region of Dalmanutha.

THE PHARISEES ASK FOR A SIGN FROM HEAVEN
(MATTHEW 16:1–4) ~see also Mark 8:11–13~

The Pharisees and Sadducees came to test Jesus. So they asked him to show them a miraculous sign from heaven.

He responded to them, "In the evening you say that the weather will be fine because the sky is red. And in the morning you say that there will be a storm today because the sky is red and overcast. You can forecast the weather by judging the appearance of the sky, but you cannot interpret the signs of the times.

"Evil and unfaithful people look for a miraculous sign. But the only sign they will be given is that of Jonah."

Then he left them standing there and went away.

THE YEAST OF THE PHARISEES
(MATTHEW 16:5–12) ~see also Mark 8:13b–21~

The disciples had forgotten to take any bread along when they went to the other side of the Sea of Galilee.

Jesus said to them, "Be careful! Watch out for the yeast of the Pharisees and Sadducees!"

The disciples had been discussing among themselves that they had not taken any bread along.

Jesus knew about their conversation and asked, "Why are you discussing among yourselves that you don't have any bread? You have so little faith! Don't you understand yet? Don't you remember the five loaves for the five thousand and how many baskets you filled? Don't you remember the seven loaves for the four thousand and how many large baskets you filled? Why don't you understand that I wasn't talking to you about bread? Watch out for the yeast of the Pharisees and Sadducees!"

Then they understood that he didn't say to watch out for the yeast in bread, but to watch out for the teachings of the Pharisees and Sadducees.

JESUS GIVES SIGHT TO A BLIND MAN
(MARK 8:22–26)

As they came to Bethsaida, some people brought a blind man to Jesus. They begged Jesus to touch him. Jesus took the blind man's hand and led him out of the village. He spit into the man's eyes and placed his hands on him. Jesus asked him, "Can you see anything?"

The man looked up and said, "I see people. They look like trees walking around."

Then Jesus placed his hands on the man's eyes a second time, and the man saw clearly. His sight was normal again. He could see everything clearly even at a distance. Jesus told him when he sent him home, "Don't go into the village."

JESUS TRAVELS NORTH TO CAESAREA PHILIPPI

Peter's faith soars to the peaks in this powerful passage where he publicly proclaims Jesus as the Messiah. Yet, moments later Peter's moment of glory is dashed to pieces in the midst of his confusion regarding Jesus'

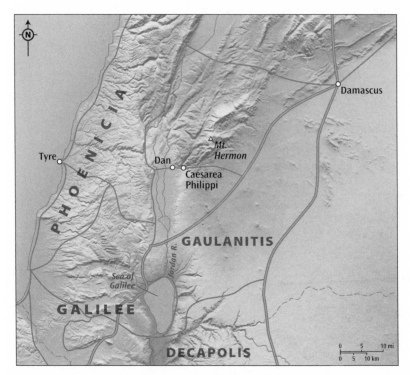

Mt. Hermon and Caesarea Philippi

impending death and resurrection. Peter may have been impetuous, and he may have misunderstood Jesus' mission here on earth, but one thing he got absolutely right was Jesus' true identity. Fully man and fully God, Jesus was indeed the Messiah, the fulfillment of all the Old Testament promises, and the hope for the world.

PETER DECLARES HIS BELIEF ABOUT JESUS
(MATTHEW 16:13–20) ~see also Mark 8:27–30 and Luke 9:18–21~

When Jesus came to the region of Caesarea Philippi, he asked his disciples, "Who do people say the Son of Man is?"

They answered, "Some say you are John the Baptizer, others Elijah, still others Jeremiah or one of the prophets."

He asked them, "But who do you say I am?"

Simon Peter answered, "You are the Messiah, the Son of the living God!"

Jesus replied, "Simon, son of Jonah, you are blessed! No human revealed this to you, but my Father in heaven revealed it to you. You are Peter, and I can guarantee that on this rock I will build my church. And the gates of hell will not overpower it. I will give you the keys of the kingdom of heaven. Whatever you imprison, God will imprison. And whatever you set free, God will set free."

Then he strictly ordered the disciples not to tell anyone that he was the Messiah.

JESUS FORETELLS THAT HE WILL
DIE AND COME BACK TO LIFE
(MATTHEW 16:21–23) ~see also Mark 8:31–33; Luke 9:22~

From that time on Jesus began to inform his disciples that he had to go to Jerusalem. There he would have to suffer a lot because of the leaders, chief priests, and scribes. He would be killed, but on the third day he would be brought back to life.

Peter took him aside and objected to this. He said, "Heaven forbid, Lord! This must never happen to you!"

But Jesus turned and said to Peter, "Get out of my way, Satan! You are tempting me to sin. You aren't thinking the way God thinks but the way humans think."

Jesus Predicts His Death

Although the Old Testament contains prophecies regarding the idea of a suffering servant, there is no evidence that the people were expecting the Messiah to be killed and resurrected. There was absolutely no precedent for such an incredible miracle, and we cannot fault the disciples for failing to grasp what Jesus was telling them. In fact, their confusion highlights the incredible nature of the resurrection. These disciples would not have thought to steal the body and invent the resurrection since they themselves could hardly believe it was going to happen. Even though the Jews looked for a Messiah, they had never expected that he would come to serve and not be served, to be humiliated and subjected to human ridicule, and ultimately suffer the same fate usually reserved for thieves and murderers. They had hoped for a mighty king, and it is understandable that even the disciples were quite confused by Jesus' repeated emphasis on his coming death.

WHAT IT MEANS TO FOLLOW JESUS
(MATTHEW 16:24–28) ~see also Mark 8:34–9:1; Luke 9:23–27~

Then Jesus said to his disciples, "Those who want to come with me must say no to the things they want, pick up their crosses, and follow me. Those who want to save their lives will lose them. But those who lose their lives for me will find them. What good will it do for people to win the whole world and lose their lives? Or what will a person give in exchange for life? The Son of Man will come with his angels in his Father's glory. Then he will pay back each person based on what that person has done. I can guarantee this truth: Some people who are standing here will not die until they see the Son of Man coming in his kingdom."

JESUS IS TRANSFIGURED ON THE MOUNTAIN

The powerful experience of the transfiguration has clear ties with the meeting between Moses and God on Mount Sinai (Exodus 24). Although in our culture we might consider this as "just another Old Testament reference," for the Jewish people the exodus was a defining moment in their history. The book of Exodus was not just one more book among many; it was one of the foundational documents of their history, faith, and identity. The exodus from Egypt was a turning point for the people, as God used Moses to create for himself the nation of Israel. The life, death, and resurrection of Jesus is another monumental turning point in God's plan for the world, and the transfiguration marks the moment in stunning fashion.

MOSES AND ELIJAH APPEAR WITH JESUS
(MATTHEW 17:1–13) ~see also Mark 9:2–13; Luke 9:28–36~

After six days Jesus took Peter, James, and John (the brother of James) and led them up a high mountain where they could be alone.

Jesus' appearance changed in front of them. His face became as bright as the sun and his clothes as white as light. Suddenly, Moses and Elijah appeared to them and were talking with Jesus.

Peter said to Jesus, "Lord, it's good that we're here. If you want, I'll put up three tents here—one for you, one for Moses, and one for Elijah."

He was still speaking when a bright cloud overshadowed them. Then a voice came out of the cloud and said, "This is my Son, whom I love and with whom I am pleased. Listen to him!"

The disciples were terrified when they heard this and fell facedown on the ground. But Jesus touched them and said, "Get up, and don't be afraid!" As they raised their heads, they saw no one but Jesus.

On their way down the mountain, Jesus ordered them, "Don't tell anyone what you have seen. Wait until the Son of Man has been brought back to life."

So the disciples asked him, "Why do the scribes say that Elijah must come first?"

Jesus answered, "Elijah is coming and will put everything in order again. Actually, I can guarantee that Elijah has already come. Yet, people treated him as they pleased because they didn't recognize him. In the same way they're going to make the Son of Man suffer."

Then the disciples understood that he was talking about John the Baptizer.

The Law and the Prophets

Moses was the author of the Pentateuch (the core documents of the Jewish faith), the one who led the people out of Egypt and brought them to the edge of the Promised Land, the one who received the Law and instituted every major aspect of Jewish worship. Elijah was a great prophet at a key moment in Israel's history; he never died but was caught up to heaven in a chariot of fire. Both Moses and Elijah had powerful experiences directly with God. For Moses it was at Sinai, for Elijah, at Mount Horeb. They quite possibly represent "the Law (Moses) and the Prophets (Elijah)," a common designation used to refer to the Old Testament. The meeting then affirms Jesus as the fulfillment and culmination of all that had come previously in the history of Israel.

JESUS CURES A DEMON-POSSESSED BOY
(MARK 9:14–29) ~see also Matthew 17:14–20; Luke 9:37–43a~

When they came to the other disciples, they saw a large crowd around them. Some scribes were arguing with them. All the people were very surprised to see Jesus and ran to welcome him.

Jesus asked the scribes, "What are you arguing about with them?"

A man in the crowd answered, "Teacher, I brought you my son. He is possessed by a spirit that won't let him talk. Whenever the spirit brings on a seizure, it throws him to the ground. Then he foams at the mouth, grinds his teeth, and becomes exhausted. I asked your disciples to force the spirit out, but they didn't have the power to do it."

Jesus said to them, "You unbelieving generation! How long must I be with you? How long must I put up with you? Bring him to me!"

They brought the boy to him. As soon as the spirit saw Jesus, it threw the boy into convulsions. He fell on the ground, rolled around, and foamed at the mouth.

Jesus asked his father, "How long has he been like this?"

The father replied, "He has been this way since he was a child. The demon has often thrown him into fire or into water to destroy him. If it's possible for you, put yourself in our place, and help us!"

Jesus said to him, "As far as possibilities go, everything is possible for the person who believes."

The child's father cried out at once, "I believe! Help my lack of faith."

When Jesus saw that a crowd was running to the scene, he gave an order to the evil spirit. He said, "You spirit that won't let him talk, I command you to come out of him and never enter him again."

The evil spirit screamed, shook the child violently, and came out. The boy looked as if he were dead, and everyone said, "He's dead!"

Jesus took his hand and helped him to stand up.

When Jesus went into a house, his disciples asked him privately, "Why couldn't we force the spirit out of the boy?"

He told them, "This kind of spirit can be forced out only by prayer."

JESUS SPENDS TIME WITH HIS DISCIPLES

As Jesus prepares for the end of his ministry, he spends some intensely focused time with the disciples, doing everything he can to prepare them for their future role as the leaders of the early church. His teaching is careful and precise, explaining the need for humility and the place of suffering, the practicalities of what would come to be called "church discipline," the crucial importance of forgiveness as an underlying current in everything they do, and the inevitable separation that their faith would cause even within their own families. The road ahead would be very hard, and Jesus equips the disciples with everything they will need to travel on it.

JESUS AGAIN FORETELLS THAT HE WILL DIE AND COME BACK TO LIFE
(MARK 9:30–32) ~*see also Matthew 17:22–23; Luke 9:43b–45*~

They left that place and were passing through Galilee. Jesus did not want anyone to know where he was because he was teaching his disciples. He taught them, "The Son of Man will be betrayed and handed over to people. They will kill him, but on the third day he will come back to life."

The disciples didn't understand what he meant and were afraid to ask him.

PAYING THE TEMPLE TAX
(MATTHEW 17:24–27)

When they came to Capernaum, the collectors of the temple tax came to Peter. They asked him, "Doesn't your teacher pay the temple tax?"

"Certainly," he answered.

Peter went into the house. Before he could speak, Jesus asked him, "What do you think, Simon? From whom do the kings of the world collect fees or taxes? Is it from their family members or from other people?"

"From other people," Peter answered.

Jesus said to him, "Then the family members are exempt. However, so that we don't create a scandal, go to the sea and throw in a hook. Take the first fish that you catch. Open its mouth, and you will find a coin. Give that coin to them for you and me."

GREATNESS IN THE KINGDOM
(MARK 9:33–41) ~see also Matthew 18:1–5; Luke 9:46–50~

Then they came to Capernaum. While Jesus was at home, he asked the disciples, "What were you arguing about on the road?" They were silent. On the road they had argued about who was the greatest.

He sat down and called the twelve apostles. He told them, "Whoever wants to be the most important person must take the last place and be a servant to everyone else." Then he took a little child and had him stand among them. He put his arms around the child and said to them, "Whoever welcomes a child like this in my name welcomes me. Whoever welcomes me welcomes not me but the one who sent me."

John said to Jesus, "Teacher, we saw someone forcing demons out of a person by using the power and authority of your name. We tried to stop him because he was not one of us."

Jesus said, "Don't stop him! No one who works a miracle in my name can turn around and speak evil of me. Whoever isn't against us is for us. I can guarantee this truth: Whoever gives you a cup of water to drink because you belong to Christ will certainly not lose his reward."

The True Kingdom

Down through history kingdoms have risen and fallen based on traditional power structures of authority and might. A king rules over his people, and they obey him absolutely or face the consequences. At the time of Jesus the Romans ruled the known world with a mighty army and a strong, visible presence in every town and city. When Jesus came talking about kingdoms, the disciples must have had difficulty thinking of anything other than a similar kingdom, with Jesus as the head. Yet, something was radically different with Jesus' kingdom vision. Instead of being served, he came to serve. He said the first was to be last, and the last first. The poor would inherit the earth. The hungry would be fed. The persecuted would receive the kingdom of heaven.

The kingdom of God is not some souped-up version of the fallen world we have created. The kingdom of God is radically different, radically other, and almost impossible to understand or enjoy without the Holy Spirit living within us, spurring us on to serve with humility under the banner of Jesus Christ, the suffering servant.

CAUSING OTHERS TO LOSE FAITH
(MARK 9:42–50) *~see also Matthew 18:6–10; Luke 17:1–4~*

"These little ones believe in me. It would be best for the person who causes one of them to lose faith to be thrown into the sea with a large stone hung around his neck.

"So if your hand causes you to lose your faith, cut it off! It is better for you to enter life disabled than to have two hands and go to hell, to the fire that cannot be put out. [Some manuscripts add: In hell worms that eat the body never die, and the fire is never put out.] If your foot causes you to lose your faith, cut it off! It is better for you to enter life lame than to have two feet and be thrown into hell. If your eye causes you to lose your faith, tear it out! It is better for you to enter the kingdom of God with one eye than to have two eyes and be thrown into hell. In hell worms that eat the body never die, and the fire is never put out. Everyone will be salted with fire. Salt is good. But if salt loses its taste, how will you restore its flavor? Have salt within you, and live in peace with one another."

DEALING WITH BELIEVERS WHEN THEY DO WRONG
(MATTHEW 18:15–20)

"If a believer does something wrong, go, confront him when the two of you are alone. If he listens to you, you have won back that believer. But if he does not listen, take one or two others with you so that every accusation may be verified by two or three witnesses. If he ignores these witnesses, tell it to the community of believers. If he also ignores the community, deal with him as you would a heathen or a tax collector. I can guarantee this truth: Whatever you imprison, God will imprison. And whatever you set free, God will set free.

"I can guarantee again that if two of you agree on anything here on earth, my Father in heaven will accept it. Where two or three have come together in my name, I am there among them."

PERSONALLY FORGIVING OTHERS
(MATTHEW 18:21–35)

Then Peter came to Jesus and asked him, "Lord, how often do I have to forgive a believer who wrongs me? Seven times?"

Jesus answered him, "I tell you, not just seven times, but seventy times seven.

"That is why the kingdom of heaven is like a king who wanted to settle accounts with his servants. When he began to do this, a servant who owed him millions of dollars was brought to him. Because he could not pay off the debt, the master ordered him, his wife, his children, and all that he had to be sold to pay off the account. Then the servant fell at his master's feet and said, 'Be patient with me, and I will repay everything!'

"The master felt sorry for his servant, freed him, and canceled his debt. But when that servant went away, he found a servant who owed him hundreds of dollars. He grabbed the servant he found and began to choke him. 'Pay what you owe!' he said.

"Then that other servant fell at his feet and begged him, 'Be patient with me, and I will repay you.' But he refused. Instead, he turned away and had that servant put into prison until he would repay what he owed.

"The other servants who worked with him saw what had happened and felt very sad. They told their master the whole story.

"Then his master sent for him and said to him, 'You evil servant! I canceled your entire debt, because you begged me. Shouldn't you have treated the other servant as mercifully as I treated you?'

"His master was so angry that he handed him over to the torturers until he would repay everything that he owed. That is what my Father in heaven will do to you if each of you does not sincerely forgive other believers."

JESUS' BROTHERS RIDICULE HIM
(JOHN 7:1–10)

Jesus later traveled throughout Galilee. He didn't want to travel in Judea because Jews there wanted to kill him.

The time for the Jewish Festival of Booths was near. So Jesus' brothers told him, "Leave this place, and go to Judea so that your disciples can see the things that you're doing. No one does things secretly when he wants to be known publicly. If you do these things, you should let the world see you." Even his brothers didn't believe in him.

Jesus told them, "Now is not the right time for me to go. Any time is right for you. The world cannot hate you, but it hates me because I say that what everyone does is evil. Go to the festival. I'm not going to this festival right now. Now is not the right time for me to go."

After saying this, Jesus stayed in Galilee. But after his brothers had gone to the festival, Jesus went. He didn't go publicly but secretly.

JESUS TRAVELS TO JERUSALEM A FINAL TIME

The road to Jerusalem marks the beginning of the end for Jesus. From this point on, his practical ministry among the people is essentially over and

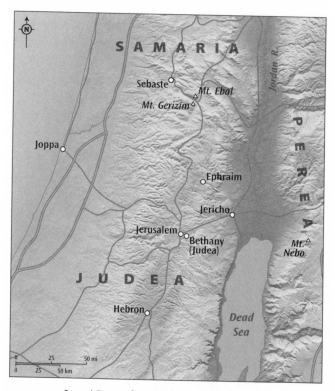

Jesus' Route from Samaria to Jerusalem

he moves into a stronger teaching role, addressing larger crowds of people in Jerusalem and engaging the Pharisees and religious leaders in debate about the Law and the Prophets. Announcing himself again as the living water (recalling his encounter with the woman at the well), Jesus causes an outcry when he speaks of himself using the divine name, "Before Abraham was ever born, I am." Forced to make a decision about his identity, the religious leaders could not fathom that Jesus truly was who he said he was, and ultimately it would be the charge of blasphemy that would lead to his crucifixion.

PEOPLE FROM A SAMARITAN VILLAGE REJECT JESUS
(LUKE 9:51–56)

The time was coming closer for Jesus to be taken to heaven. So he was determined to go to Jerusalem. He sent messengers ahead of him. They went into a Samaritan village to arrange a place for him to stay. But the people didn't welcome him, because he was on his way to Jerusalem. James and John, his disciples, saw this. They asked, "Lord, do you want us to call down fire from heaven to burn them up?"

But he turned and corrected them. So they went to another village.

WHAT IT TAKES TO BE A DISCIPLE
(LUKE 9:57–62) ~see also Matthew 8:19–22~

As they were walking along the road, a man said to Jesus, "I'll follow you wherever you go."

Jesus told him, "Foxes have holes, and birds have nests, but the Son of Man has nowhere to sleep."

He told another man, "Follow me!"

But the man said, "Sir, first let me go to bury my father."

But Jesus told him, "Let the dead bury their own dead. You must go everywhere and tell about the kingdom of God."

Another said, "I'll follow you, sir, but first let me tell my family goodbye."

Jesus said to him, "Whoever starts to plow and looks back is not fit for the kingdom of God."

JESUS GOES TO THE FESTIVAL OF BOOTHS
(JOHN 7:11–53)

The Jews were looking for Jesus in the crowd at the festival. They kept asking, "Where is that man?" The crowds argued about Jesus. Some people said, "He's a good man," while others said, "No he isn't. He deceives the people." Yet, no one would talk openly about him because they were afraid of the Jews.

When the festival was half over, Jesus went to the temple courtyard and began to teach. The Jews were surprised and asked, "How can this man be so educated when he hasn't gone to school?"

Jesus responded to them, "What I teach doesn't come from me but from the one who sent me. Those who want to follow the will of God will know if what I teach is from God or if I teach my own thoughts. Those who speak their own thoughts are looking for their own glory. But the man who wants to bring glory to the one who sent him is a true teacher and doesn't have dishonest motives. Didn't Moses give you his teachings? Yet, none of you does what Moses taught you. So why do you want to kill me?"

The crowd answered, "You're possessed by a demon! Who wants to kill you?"

Jesus answered them, "I performed one miracle, and all of you are surprised by it. Moses gave you the teaching about circumcision (although it didn't come from Moses but from our ancestors). So you circumcise a male on a day of worship. If you circumcise a male on the day of worship to follow Moses' Teachings, why are you angry with me because I made a man entirely well on the day of worship? Stop judging by outward appearance! Instead, judge correctly."

Some of the people who lived in Jerusalem said, "Isn't this the man they want to kill? But look at this! He's speaking in public, and no one is saying anything to him! Can it be that the rulers really know that this man is the Messiah? However, we know where this man comes from. When the Christ comes, no one will know where he is from."

Then, while Jesus was teaching in the temple courtyard, he said loudly, "You know me, and you know where I come from. I didn't decide to come on my own. The one who sent me is true. He's the one you don't know. I know him because I am from him and he sent me."

The Jews tried to arrest him but couldn't because his time had not yet come.

However, many people in the crowd believed in him. They asked, "When the Messiah comes, will he perform more miracles than this man has?"

The Pharisees heard the crowd saying things like this about him. So the chief priests and the Pharisees sent temple guards to arrest Jesus.

Jesus said, "I will still be with you for a little while. Then I'll go to the one who sent me. You will look for me, but you won't find me. You can't go where I'm going."

The Jews said among themselves, "Where does this man intend to go so that we won't find him? Does he mean that he'll live with the Jews who are scattered among the Greeks and that he'll teach the Greeks? What does he mean when he says, 'You will look for me, but you won't find me,' and 'You can't go where I'm going'?"

On the last and most important day of the festival, Jesus was standing in the temple courtyard. He said loudly, "Whoever is thirsty must come to me to drink. As Scripture says, 'Streams of living water will flow from deep within the person who believes in me.'" Jesus said this about the Spirit, whom his believers would receive. The Spirit was not yet evident, as it would be after Jesus had been glorified.

After some of the crowd heard Jesus say these words, they said, "This man is certainly the prophet." Other people said, "This man is the Messiah." Still other people asked, "How can the Messiah come from Galilee? Doesn't Scripture say that the Messiah will come from the descendants of David and from the village of Bethlehem, where David lived?" So the people were divided because of Jesus. Some of them wanted to arrest him, but they couldn't.

When the temple guards returned, the chief priests and Pharisees asked them, "Why didn't you bring Jesus?"

The temple guards answered, "No human has ever spoken like this man."

The Pharisees asked the temple guards, "Have you been deceived too? Has any ruler or any Pharisee believed in him? This crowd is cursed because it doesn't know Moses' Teachings."

One of those Pharisees was Nicodemus, who had previously visited Jesus. Nicodemus asked them, "Do Moses' Teachings enable us to judge a person without first hearing that person's side of the story? We can't judge a person without finding out what that person has done."

They asked Nicodemus, "Are you saying this because you're from Galilee? Study the Scriptures, and you'll see that no prophet comes from Galilee."

Then each of them went home.

The Festival of Booths

The Festival of Booths was the highlight of the year, the favorite of all the festivals. "The Feast," as it was often known, was a time to remember God's provision for the people as they journeyed through the desert from Egypt to the Promised Land. Held in the fall, this was a time for rejoicing, dancing, and singing of praise psalms. The Feast also involved a ritual of water—every morning the priests would go to the pool of Siloam and fill their jars with water, which would then be poured out on the altar at the temple as an offering to God, symbolizing his life-giving provision. Jesus used this popular ritual to point the people to himself as the true source of living water.

A WOMAN CAUGHT IN ADULTERY
(JOHN 8:1–11)

Jesus went to the Mount of Olives. Early the next morning he returned to the temple courtyard. All the people went to him, so he sat down and began to teach them.

The scribes and the Pharisees brought a woman who had been caught committing adultery. They made her stand in front of everyone and asked Jesus, "Teacher, we caught this woman in the act of adultery. In his teachings, Moses ordered us to stone women like this to death. What do you say?" They asked this to test him. They wanted to find a reason to bring charges against him.

Jesus bent down and used his finger to write on the ground. When they persisted in asking him questions, he straightened up and said, "The person who is sinless should be the first to throw a stone at her." Then he bent down again and continued writing on the ground.

One by one, beginning with the older men, the scribes and Pharisees left. Jesus was left alone with the woman. Then Jesus straightened up and asked her, "Where did they go? Has anyone condemned you?"

The woman answered, "No one, sir."

Jesus said, "I don't condemn you either. Go! From now on don't sin."

JESUS SPEAKS WITH THE PHARISEES ABOUT HIS FATHER
(JOHN 8:12–59)

Jesus spoke to the Pharisees again. He said, "I am the light of the world. Whoever follows me will have a life filled with light and will never live in the dark."

The Pharisees said to him, "You testify on your own behalf, so your testimony isn't true."

Jesus replied to them, "Even if I testify on my own behalf, my testimony is true because I know where I came from and where I'm going. However, you don't know where I came from or where I'm going. You judge the way humans do. I don't judge anyone. Even if I do judge, my judgment is valid because I don't make it on my own. I make my judgment with the Father who sent me. Your own teachings say that the testimony of two people is true. I testify on my own behalf, and so does the Father who sent me."

The Pharisees asked him, "Where is your father?"

Jesus replied, "You don't know me or my Father. If you knew me, you would also know my Father."

Jesus spoke these words while he was teaching in the treasury area of the temple courtyard. No one arrested him, because his time had not yet come.

Jesus spoke to the Pharisees again. He said, "I'm going away, and you'll look for me. But you will die because of your sin. You can't go where I'm going."

Then the Jews asked, "Is he going to kill himself? Is that what he means when he says, 'You can't go where I'm going'?"

Jesus said to them, "You're from below. I'm from above. You're from this world. I'm not from this world. For this reason I told you that you'll die because of your sins. If you don't believe that I am the one, you'll die because of your sins."

The Jews asked him, "Who did you say you are?"

Jesus told them, "I am who I said I was from the beginning. I have a lot I could say about you and a lot I could condemn you for. But the one who sent me is true. So I tell the world exactly what he has told me." (The Jews didn't know that he was talking to them about the Father.)

So Jesus told them, "When you have lifted up the Son of Man, then you'll know that I am the one and that I can't do anything on my own. Instead, I speak as the Father taught me. Besides, the one who sent me is with me. He hasn't left me by myself. I always do what pleases him."

As Jesus was saying this, many people believed in him. So Jesus said to those Jews who believed in him, "If you live by what I say, you are truly my disciples. You will know the truth, and the truth will set you free."

They replied to Jesus, "We are Abraham's descendants, and we've never been anyone's slaves. So how can you say that we will be set free?"

Jesus answered them, "I can guarantee this truth: Whoever lives a sinful life is a slave to sin. A slave doesn't live in the home forever, but a son does. So if the Son sets you free, you will be absolutely free. I know that you're Abraham's descendants. However, you want to kill me because you don't like what I'm saying. What I'm saying is what I have seen in my Father's presence. But you do what you've heard from your father."

The Jews replied to Jesus, "Abraham is our father."

Jesus told them, "If you were Abraham's children, you would do what Abraham did. I am a man who has told you the truth that I heard from God. But now you want to kill me. Abraham wouldn't have done that. You're doing what your father does."

The Jews said to Jesus, "We're not illegitimate children. God is our only Father."

Jesus told them, "If God were your Father, you would love me. After all, I'm here, and I came from God. I didn't come on my own. Instead, God sent me. Why don't you understand the language I use? Is it because you can't understand the words I use? You come from your father, the devil, and you desire to do what your father wants you to do. The devil was a murderer from the beginning. He has never been truthful. He doesn't know what the truth is. Whenever he tells a lie, he's doing what comes naturally to him. He's a liar and the father of lies. So you don't believe me because I tell the truth. Can any of you convict me of committing a sin? If I'm telling the truth, why don't you believe me? The person who belongs to God understands what God says. You don't understand because you don't belong to God."

The Jews replied to Jesus, "Aren't we right when we say that you're a Samaritan and that you're possessed by a demon?"

Jesus answered, "I'm not possessed. I honor my Father, but you dishonor me. I don't want my own glory. But there is someone who wants it, and he is the judge. I can guarantee this truth: Whoever obeys what I say will never see death."

The Jews told Jesus, "Now we know that you're possessed by a demon. Abraham died, and so did the prophets, but you say, 'Whoever does what I say will never taste death.' Are you greater than our father Abraham, who died? The prophets have also died. Who do you think you are?"

Jesus said, "If I bring glory to myself, my glory is nothing. My Father is the one who gives me glory, and you say that he is your God. Yet, you haven't known him. However, I know him. If I would say that I didn't know him, I would be a liar like all of you. But I do know him, and I do what he says. Your father Abraham was pleased to see that my day was coming. He saw it and was happy."

The Jews said to Jesus, "You're not even fifty years old. How could you have seen Abraham?"

Jesus told them, "I can guarantee this truth: Before Abraham was ever born, I am."

Then some of the Jews picked up stones to throw at Jesus. However, Jesus was concealed, and he left the temple courtyard.

JESUS SENDS DISCIPLES TO DO MISSION WORK
(LUKE 10:1–24)

After this, the Lord appointed 70 other disciples to go ahead of him to every city and place that he intended to go. They were to travel in pairs.

He told them, "The harvest is large, but the workers are few. So ask the Lord who gives this harvest to send workers to harvest his crops. Go! I'm sending you out like lambs among wolves. Don't carry a wallet, a traveling bag, or sandals, and don't stop to greet anyone on the way. Whenever you go into a house, greet the family right away with the words, 'May there be peace in this house.' If a peaceful person lives there, your greeting will be accepted. But if that's not the case, your greeting will be rejected. Stay with the family that accepts you. Eat and drink whatever they offer you. After all, the worker deserves his pay. Do not move around from one house to another. Whenever you go into a city and the people welcome you, eat whatever they serve you. Heal the sick that are there, and tell the people, 'The kingdom of God is near you!'

"But whenever you go into a city and people don't welcome you, leave. Announce in its streets, 'We are wiping your city's dust from our feet in protest against you! But realize that the kingdom of God is near you!' I can guarantee that judgment day will be easier for Sodom than for that city.

"How horrible it will be for you, Chorazin! How horrible it will be for you, Bethsaida! If the miracles worked in your cities had been worked in Tyre and Sidon, they would have changed the way they thought and acted. Long ago they would have worn sackcloth and sat in ashes. Judgment day will be better for Tyre and Sidon than for you. And you, Capernaum, will you be lifted to heaven? No, you will go to hell!

"The person who hears you hears me, and the person who rejects you rejects me. The person who rejects me rejects the one who sent me."

The 70 disciples came back very happy. They said, "Lord, even demons obey us when we use the power and authority of your name!"

Jesus said to them, "I watched Satan fall from heaven like lightning. I have given you the authority to trample snakes and scorpions and to destroy the enemy's power. Nothing will hurt you. However, don't be happy that evil spirits obey you. Be happy that your names are written in heaven."

In that hour the Holy Spirit filled Jesus with joy. Jesus said, "I praise you, Father, Lord of heaven and earth, for hiding these things from wise and intelligent people and revealing them to little children. Yes, Father, this is what pleased you.

"My Father has turned everything over to me. Only the Father knows who the Son is. And no one knows who the Father is except the Son and those to whom the Son is willing to reveal him."

He turned to his disciples in private and said to them, "How blessed you are to see what you've seen. I can guarantee that many prophets and kings wanted to see and hear what you've seen and heard, but they didn't."

JESUS TELLS STORIES TO THE PEOPLE

Luke contains a substantial amount of material that is unique to his Gospel. Centered around teachings regarding the kingdom of God and placed chronologically during Jesus' final journey toward Jerusalem, these stories are often surprising in their subject matter and startling in the way they turned the traditional religious system on its head. The Good Samaritan and the Prodigal Son are powerful commentaries on God's deep love for his people. Jesus' teaching on discipleship, although hard to understand at the time, set a model followed by the apostles and preached with authority through their letters. Jesus' profound challenges to a culture based on material wealth resonate at a deep level in contemporary Western cultures ruled by money and possessions. Whatever the subject matter, Jesus used every opportunity to point people toward God and push them deeper in their relationship with him.

A STORY ABOUT A GOOD SAMARITAN
(LUKE 10:25–37)

Then an expert in Moses' Teachings stood up to test Jesus. He asked, "Teacher, what must I do to inherit eternal life?"

Jesus answered him, "What is written in Moses' Teachings? What do you read there?"

He answered, "'Love the Lord your God with all your heart, with all your soul, with all your strength, and with all your mind.' And love your neighbor as you love yourself.'"

Jesus told him, "You're right! Do this, and life will be yours."

But the man wanted to justify his question. So he asked Jesus, "Who is my neighbor?"

Jesus replied, "A man went from Jerusalem to Jericho. On the way robbers stripped him, beat him, and left him for dead.

"By chance, a priest was traveling along that road. When he saw the man, he went around him and continued on his way. Then a Levite came to that place. When he saw the man, he, too, went around him and continued on his way.

"But a Samaritan, as he was traveling along, came across the man. When the Samaritan saw him, he felt sorry for the man, went to him, and cleaned and bandaged his wounds. Then he put him on his own animal, brought him to an inn, and took care of him. The next day the Samaritan took out two silver coins and gave them to the innkeeper. He told the innkeeper, 'Take care of him. If you spend more than that, I'll pay you on my return trip.'

"Of these three men, who do you think was a neighbor to the man who was attacked by robbers?"

The expert said, "The one who was kind enough to help him."

Jesus told him, "Go and imitate his example!"

The Good Samaritan

In order to understand this story we have to be clear about the principal characters involved. The priest was exactly that—someone serving in the temple on a regular basis; many priests, however, also lived outside the city, hence his travel on the road to Jericho. The Levite was not a priest but a helper to the priests. Their combined failure to help was no doubt representative of the failure of the priestly class to share God's heart of compassion and justice for the poor and needy. The Old Testament prophets are filled with stinging rebukes directed toward God's people for their failure to care for the poor. This parable has a similar air to it. The Samaritan is the odd one out. He was a member of a despised race and considered to be on the same par as Gentiles; it was unthinkable for a Jew to cast a Samaritan as the good guy in the story. The story was not just about helping others and would have been absolutely shocking in its content to any original hearer.

MARY LISTENS TO JESUS
(LUKE 10:38–42)

As they were traveling along, Jesus went into a village. A woman named Martha welcomed him into her home. She had a sister named Mary. Mary sat at the Lord's feet and listened to him talk.

But Martha was upset about all the work she had to do. So she asked, "Lord, don't you care that my sister has left me to do the work all by myself? Tell her to help me."

The Lord answered her, "Martha, Martha! You worry and fuss about a lot of things. There's only one thing you need. Mary has made the right choice, and that one thing will not be taken away from her."

THE POWER OF PRAYER
(LUKE 11:5–13) ~see also Matthew 7:7–11~

Jesus said to his disciples, "Suppose one of you has a friend. Suppose you go to him at midnight and say, 'Friend, let me borrow three loaves of bread. A friend of mine on a trip has dropped in on me, and I don't have anything to serve him.' Your friend might answer you from inside his house, 'Don't bother me! The door is already locked, and my children are in bed. I can't get up to give you anything.' I can guarantee that although he doesn't want to get up to give you anything, he will get up and give you whatever you need because he is your friend and because you were so bold.

"So I tell you to ask, and you will receive. Search, and you will find. Knock, and the door will be opened for you. Everyone who asks will receive. The one who searches will find, and for the person who knocks, the door will be opened.

"If your child asks you, his father, for a fish, would you give him a snake instead? Or if your child asks you for an egg, would you give him a scorpion? Even though you're evil, you know how to give good gifts to your children. So how much more will your Father in heaven give the Holy Spirit to those who ask him?"

Answered Prayers

Jesus said, "Everyone who asks will receive." That seems to imply that everything we ask for will happen, yet any Christian will tell you that this absolute claim doesn't always match up with his or her actual experience. What is clear is that God delights to answer our prayers. As the examples Jesus gives attest, if *we* know how to give good gifts to our children, doesn't God? The disconnect is perhaps most often felt because there is sometimes a dramatic difference between what we think we want and what God knows we need. While we might like a life of ease and comfort, with all needs taken care of, we live in a fallen world and the overall message of the Bible is that followers of God are to expect suffering and persecution now, although heavenly rewards await us in the afterlife.

JESUS TALKS ABOUT LIGHT
(LUKE 11:33–36)

"No one lights a lamp and hides it or puts it under a basket. Instead, everyone who lights a lamp puts it on a lamp stand so that those who come in will see its light.

"Your eye is the lamp of your body. When your eye is unclouded, your whole body is full of light. But when your eye is evil, your body is full of darkness. So be careful that the light in you isn't darkness. If your whole body is full of light and not darkness, it will be as bright as a lamp shining on you."

JESUS CRITICIZES SOME JEWISH LEADERS
(LUKE 11:37–54)

After Jesus spoke, a Pharisee invited him to have lunch at his house. So Jesus accepted the invitation. The Pharisee was surprised to see that Jesus didn't wash before the meal.

The Lord said to him, "You Pharisees clean the outside of cups and dishes. But inside you are full of greed and evil. You fools! Didn't the one who made the outside make the inside too? Give what is inside as a gift to the poor, and then everything will be clean for you.

"How horrible it will be for you Pharisees! You give God one-tenth of your mint, spices, and every garden herb. But you have ignored justice and the love of God. You should have done these things without ignoring the others.

"How horrible it will be for you Pharisees! You love to sit in the front seats in the synagogues and to be greeted in the marketplaces. How horrible it will be for you! You are like unmarked graves. People walk on them without knowing what they are."

One of the experts in Moses' Teachings said to him, "Teacher, when you talk this way, you insult us too."

Jesus said, "How horrible it will be for you experts in Moses' Teachings! You burden people with loads that are hard to carry. But you won't lift a finger to carry any of these loads.

"How horrible it will be for you! You build the monuments for the prophets. But it was your ancestors who murdered them. So you are witnesses and approve of what your ancestors did. They murdered the prophets for whom you build monuments. That's why the Wisdom of God said, 'I will send them prophets and apostles. They will murder some of those prophets and apostles and persecute others.' So the people living now will be charged with the murder of every prophet since the world was made. This includes the murders from Abel to Zechariah, who was killed between the altar and the temple. Yes, I can guarantee this truth: The people living today will be held responsible for this.

"How horrible it will be for you experts in Moses' Teachings! You have taken away the key that unlocks knowledge. You haven't gained entrance into knowledge yourselves, and you've kept out those who wanted to enter."

When Jesus left, the scribes and the Pharisees held a terrible grudge against him. They questioned him about many things and watched him closely to trap him in something he might say.

JESUS SPEAKS TO HIS DISCIPLES
(LUKE 12:1–12)

Meanwhile, thousands of people had gathered. They were so crowded that they stepped on each other. Jesus spoke to his disciples and said, "Watch out for the yeast of the Pharisees. I'm talking about their hypocrisy. Nothing has been covered that will not be exposed. Whatever is secret will be made known. Whatever you have said in the dark will be heard in the daylight. Whatever you have whispered in private rooms will be shouted from the housetops.

"My friends, I can guarantee that you don't need to be afraid of those who kill the body. After that they can't do anything more. I'll show you the one you should be afraid of. Be afraid of the one who has the power to throw you into hell after killing you. I'm warning you to be afraid of him.

"Aren't five sparrows sold for two cents? God doesn't forget any of them. Even every hair on your head has been counted. Don't be afraid! You are worth more than many sparrows. I can guarantee that the Son of Man will acknowledge in front of God's angels every person who acknowledges him in front of others. But God's angels will be told that I don't know those people who tell others that they don't know me. Everyone who says something against the Son of Man will be forgiven. But the person who dishonors the Holy Spirit will not be forgiven.

"When you are put on trial in synagogues or in front of rulers and authorities, don't worry about how you will defend yourselves or what you will say. At that time the Holy Spirit will teach you what you must say."

"Every Hair on Your Head"

It's easy to believe God has the big picture taken care of, but what about the little details? Does he *really* know how many hair follicles I have? What's the point in that? Within the context of the passage, Jesus is training his disciples for future ministry, preparing them for the work that lies ahead for them once he has gone. The central element of his message is that they are going to face suffering, persecution, and maybe even death for their beliefs. Yet, through it all they are to hold firm to God's sovereignty over all things. Ultimately, whatever happens to the disciples, God will triumph. They can take comfort knowing that they are made in the image of God, created and imbued with special gifts and abilities, and known personally by the living God. That God knows every hair on their head is both a metaphor describing God's love for them and a reality describing the omniscience of the God who made all things and holds all things together.

A STORY ABOUT MATERIAL POSSESSIONS
(LUKE 12:13–21)

Someone in the crowd said to him, "Teacher, tell my brother to give me my share of the inheritance that our father left us."

Jesus said to him, "Who appointed me to be your judge or to divide your inheritance?"

He told the people, "Be careful to guard yourselves from every kind of greed. Life is not about having a lot of material possessions."

Then he used this illustration. He said, "A rich man had land that produced good crops. He thought, 'What should I do? I don't have enough room to store my crops.' He said, 'I know what I'll do. I'll tear down my barns and build bigger ones so that I can store all my grain and goods in them. Then I'll say to myself, "You've stored up a lot of good things for years to come. Take life easy, eat, drink, and enjoy yourself."'

"But God said to him, 'You fool! I will demand your life from you tonight! Now who will get what you've accumulated?' That's how it is when a person has material riches but is not rich in his relationship with God."

STOP WORRYING
(LUKE 12:22–34) ~see also Matthew 6:25–34~

Then Jesus said to his disciples, "So I tell you to stop worrying about what you will eat or wear. Life is more than food, and the body is more than clothes. Consider the crows. They don't plant or harvest. They don't even have a storeroom or a barn. Yet, God feeds them. You are worth much more than birds.

"Can any of you add an hour to your life by worrying? If you can't do a small thing like that, why worry about other things? Consider how the flowers grow. They never work or spin yarn for clothes. But I say that not even Solomon in all his majesty was dressed like one of these flowers. That's the way God clothes the grass in the field. Today it's alive, and tomorrow it's thrown into an incinerator. So how much more will he clothe you people who have so little faith?

"Don't concern yourself about what you will eat or drink, and quit worrying about these things. Everyone in the world is concerned about these things, but your Father knows you need them. Rather, be concerned about his kingdom. Then these things will be provided for you. Don't be afraid, little flock. Your Father is pleased to give you the kingdom.

"Sell your material possessions, and give the money to the poor. Make yourselves wallets that don't wear out! Make a treasure for yourselves in heaven that never loses its value! In heaven thieves and moths can't get close enough to destroy your treasure. Your heart will be where your treasure is."

THE SON OF MAN WILL RETURN WHEN YOU LEAST EXPECT HIM
(LUKE 12:35–59)

"Be ready for action, and have your lamps burning. Be like servants waiting to open the door at their master's knock when he returns from a wedding. Blessed are those servants whom the master finds awake when he comes. I can guarantee this truth: He will change his clothes, make them sit down at the table, and serve them. They will be blessed if he comes in the middle of the night or toward morning and finds them awake.

"Of course, you realize that if the homeowner had known at what hour the thief was coming, he would not have let him break into his house. Be ready, because the Son of Man will return when you least expect him."

Peter asked, "Lord, did you use this illustration just for us or for everyone?"

The Lord asked, "Who, then, is the faithful, skilled manager that the master will put in charge of giving the other servants their share of food at the right time? That servant will be blessed if his master finds him doing this job when he comes. I can guarantee this truth: He will put that servant in charge of all his property. On the other hand, that servant may think that his master is taking a long time to come home. The servant may begin to beat the other servants and to eat, drink, and get drunk. His master will return at an unexpected time. Then his master will punish him severely and assign him a place with unfaithful people.

"The servant who knew what his master wanted but didn't get ready to do it will receive a hard beating. But the servant who didn't know what his master wanted and did things for which he deserved punishment will receive a light beating. A lot will be expected from everyone who has been given a lot. More will be demanded from everyone who has been entrusted with a lot.

"I have come to throw fire on the earth. I wish that it had already started! I have a baptism to go through, and I will suffer until it is over.

"Do you think I came to bring peace to earth? No! I can guarantee that I came to bring nothing but division. From now on a family of five will be divided. Three will be divided against two and two against three. A father will be against his son and a son against his father. A mother will be against her daughter and a daughter against her mother. A mother-in-law will be against her daughter-in-law and a daughter-in-law against her mother-in-law."

Jesus said to the crowds, "When you see a cloud coming up in the west, you immediately say, 'There's going to be a rainstorm,' and it happens. When you see a south wind blowing, you say, 'It's going to be hot,' and that's what happens. You hypocrites! You can forecast the weather by judging the appearance of earth and sky. But for some reason you don't know how to judge the time in which you're living. So why don't you judge for yourselves what is right? For instance, when an opponent brings you to court in front of a ruler, do your best to settle with him before you get there. Otherwise, he will drag you in front of a judge. The judge will hand you over to an officer who will throw you into prison. I can guarantee that you won't get out until you pay every penny of your fine."

Jesus' Return

David Pao and Ekhard Schnabel, professors of New Testament at Trinity Evangelical Divinity School, have noted that there are clear allusions in this passage both to the Passover narrative of Exodus 12 and the endtimes prophecy of Habakkuk 2. (G. K. Beale and D. A. Carson, eds; *Commentary on the New Testament Use of the Old Testament* [Grand Rapids: Baker, 2007] pp. 331-332.) The Passover is called to mind by the stress placed on being prepared for that day. As the Israelites were told to eat with their staff in their hands, ready to leave Egypt at a moment's notice, so too Jesus calls on his believers to live in constant anticipation of his return. They are to resist the lure of this world that suggests they take things easy and set aside their devotion to the Lord. Instead they are to be like the wise and skillful manager who was ready for his master's return. The point is not to discern when Jesus is coming back, but to focus attention on how we are to live today as we wait.

JESUS TELLS PEOPLE TO TURN TO GOD AND CHANGE THE WAY THEY THINK AND ACT
(LUKE 13:1–9)

At that time some people reported to Jesus about some Galileans whom Pilate had executed while they were sacrificing animals. Jesus replied to them, "Do you think that this happened to them because they were more sinful than other people from Galilee? No! I can guarantee that they weren't. But if you don't turn to God and change the way you think and act, then you, too, will all die. What about those 18 people who died when the tower at Siloam fell on them? Do you think that they were more sinful than other people living in Jerusalem? No! I can guarantee that they weren't. But if you don't turn to God and change the way you think and act, then you, too, will all die."

Then Jesus used this illustration: "A man had a fig tree growing in his vineyard. He went to look for fruit on the tree but didn't find any. He said to the gardener, 'For the last three years I've come to look for figs on this fig tree but haven't found any. Cut it down! Why should it use up good soil?'

"The gardener replied, 'Sir, let it stand for one more year. I'll dig around it and fertilize it. Maybe next year it'll have figs. But if not, then cut it down.'"

JESUS HEALS A DISABLED WOMAN
(LUKE 13:10–17)

Jesus was teaching in a synagogue on the day of worship. A woman who was possessed by a spirit was there. The spirit had disabled her for 18 years. She was hunched over and couldn't stand up straight. When Jesus saw her, he called her to come to him and said, "Woman, you are free from your disability." He placed his hands on her, and she immediately stood up straight and praised God.

The synagogue leader was irritated with Jesus for healing on the day of worship. The leader told the crowd, "There are six days when work can be done. So come on one of those days to be healed. Don't come on the day of worship."

The Lord said, "You hypocrites! Don't each of you free your ox or donkey on the day of worship? Don't you then take it out of its stall to give it some water to drink? Now, here is a descendant of Abraham. Satan has kept her in this condition for 18 years. Isn't it right to free her on the day of worship?"

As he said this, everyone who opposed him felt ashamed. But the entire crowd was happy about the miraculous things he was doing.

JESUS GIVES SIGHT TO A BLIND MAN
(JOHN 9:1–41)

As Jesus walked along, he saw a man who had been born blind. His disciples asked him, "Rabbi, why was this man born blind? Did he or his parents sin?"

Jesus answered, "Neither this man nor his parents sinned. Instead, he was born blind so that God could show what he can do for him. We must do what the one who sent me wants us to do while it is day. The night when no one can do anything is coming. As long as I'm in the world, I'm light for the world."

After Jesus said this, he spit on the ground and mixed the spit with dirt. Then he smeared it on the man's eyes and told him, "Wash it off in the pool of Siloam." (*Siloam* means "sent.") The blind man washed it off and returned. He was able to see.

His neighbors and those who had previously seen him begging asked, "Isn't this the man who used to sit and beg?"

Some of them said, "He's the one." Others said, "No, he isn't, but he looks like him." But the man himself said, "I am the one."

So they asked him, "How did you receive your sight?"

He replied, "The man people call Jesus mixed some spit with dirt, smeared it on my eyes, and told me, 'Go to Siloam, and wash it off.' So I went there, washed it off, and received my sight."

They asked him, "Where is that man?"

The man answered, "I don't know."

Some people brought the man who had been blind to the Pharisees. The day when Jesus mixed the spit and dirt and gave the man sight was a day of worship. So the Pharisees asked the man again how he received his sight.

The man told the Pharisees, "He put a mixture of spit and dirt on my eyes. I washed it off, and now I can see."

Some of the Pharisees said, "The man who did this is not from God because he doesn't follow the traditions for the day of worship." Other Pharisees asked, "How can a man who is a sinner perform miracles like these?" So the Pharisees were divided in their opinions.

They asked the man who had been born blind another question: "What do you say about the man who gave you sight?"

The man answered, "He's a prophet."

Until they talked to the man's parents, the Jews didn't believe that the man had been blind and had been given sight. They asked his parents, "Is this your son, the one you say was born blind? Why can he see now?"

His parents replied, "We know that he's our son and that he was born blind. But we don't know how he got his sight or who gave it to him. You'll have to ask him. He's old enough to answer for himself." (His parents said this because they were afraid of the Jews. The Jews had already agreed to put anyone who acknowledged that Jesus was the Christ out of the synagogue. That's why his parents said, "You'll have to ask him. He's old enough.")

So once again the Jews called the man who had been blind. They told him, "Give glory to God. We know that this man who gave you sight is a sinner."

The man responded, "I don't know if he's a sinner or not. But I do know one thing. I used to be blind, but now I can see."

The Jews asked him, "What did he do to you? How did he give you sight?"

The man replied, "I've already told you, but you didn't listen. Why do you want to hear the story again? Do you want to become his disciples too?"

The Jews yelled at him, "You're his disciple, but we're Moses' disciples. We know that God spoke to Moses, but we don't know where this man came from."

The man replied to them, "That's amazing! You don't know where he's from. Yet, he gave me sight. We know that God doesn't listen to sinners. Instead, he listens to people who are devout and who do what he wants. Since the beginning of time, no one has ever heard of anyone giving sight to a person born blind. If this man were not from God, he couldn't do anything like that."

The Jews answered him, "You were born full of sin. Do you think you can teach us?" Then they threw him out of the synagogue.

Jesus heard that the Jews had thrown the man out of the synagogue. So when Jesus found the man, he asked him, "Do you believe in the Son of Man?"

The man replied, "Sir, tell me who he is so that I can believe in him."

Jesus told him, "You've seen him. He is the person who is now talking with you."

The man bowed in front of Jesus and said, "I believe, Lord."

Then Jesus said, "I have come into this world to judge: Blind people will be given sight, and those who can see will become blind."

Some Pharisees who were with Jesus heard this. So they asked him, "Do you think we're blind?"

Jesus told them, "If you were blind, you wouldn't be sinners. But now you say, 'We see,' so you continue to be sinners."

JESUS, THE GOOD SHEPHERD
(JOHN 10:1–21)

"I can guarantee this truth: The person who doesn't enter the sheep pen through the gate but climbs in somewhere else is a thief or a robber. But the one who enters through the gate is the shepherd. The gatekeeper opens the gate for him, and the sheep respond to his voice. He calls his sheep by name and leads them out of the pen. After he has brought out all his sheep, he walks ahead of them. The sheep follow him because they recognize his voice. They won't follow a stranger. Instead, they will run away from a stranger because they don't recognize his voice." Jesus used this illustration as he talked to the people, but they didn't understand what he meant.

Jesus emphasized, "I can guarantee this truth: I am the gate for the sheep. All who came before I did were thieves or robbers. However, the sheep didn't respond to them. I am the gate. Those who enter the sheep pen through me will be saved. They will go in and out of the sheep pen and find food. A thief comes to steal, kill, and destroy. But I came so that my sheep will have life and so that they will have everything they need.

"I am the good shepherd. The good shepherd gives his life for the sheep. A hired hand isn't a shepherd and doesn't own the sheep. When he sees a wolf coming, he abandons the sheep and quickly runs away. So the wolf drags the sheep away and scatters the flock. The hired hand is concerned about what he's going to get paid and not about the sheep.

"I am the good shepherd. I know my sheep as the Father knows me. My sheep know me as I know the Father. So I give my life for my sheep. I also have other sheep that are not from this pen. I must lead them. They, too, will respond to my voice. So they will be one flock with one shepherd. The Father loves me because I give my life in order to take it back again. No one takes my life from me. I give my life of my own free will. I have the authority to give my life, and I have the authority to take my life back again. This is what my Father ordered me to do."

The Jews were divided because of what Jesus said. Many of them said, "He's possessed by a demon! He's crazy! Why do you listen to him?" Others said, "No one talks like this if he's possessed by a demon. Can a demon give sight to the blind?"

The Good Shepherd and His Sheep

The shepherd was a common image used by the Israelites. Reflecting the pastoral setting in much of the country, the shepherd's role was almost universally known and understood. Moreover, this was an image rich with Old Testament allusions, calling to mind both God as the ultimate good shepherd of his chosen people, Israel, and also David, the shepherd who became king. David was often referred to as a good shepherd, and he was used as a symbol by many to describe the coming Messiah. What becomes clear through this teaching is that Jesus saw himself playing a role that was completely in keeping with the people's expectations of a Davidic king as prophesied in the Old Testament. Jesus had come to care for his people and cast out those who were leading them astray. The imagery shows God's deep love for his people, a love so great that his Son would ultimately lay his life down in order to secure their salvation.

THE JEWS REJECT JESUS
(JOHN 10:22–42)

The Festival of the Dedication of the Temple took place in Jerusalem during the winter. Jesus was walking on Solomon's porch in the temple courtyard.

The Jews surrounded him. They asked him, "How long will you keep us in suspense? If you are the Messiah, tell us plainly."

Jesus answered them, "I've told you, but you don't believe me. The things that I do in my Father's name testify on my behalf. However, you don't believe because you're not my sheep. My sheep respond to my voice, and I know who they are. They follow me, and I give them eternal life. They will never be lost, and no one will tear them away from me. My Father, who gave them to me, is greater than everyone else, and no one can tear them away from my Father. The Father and I are one."

The Jews had again brought some rocks to stone Jesus to death. Jesus replied to them, "I've shown you many good things that come from the Father. For which of these good things do you want to stone me to death?"

The Jews answered Jesus, "We're going to stone you to death, not for any good things you've done, but for dishonoring God. You claim to be God, although you're only a man."

Jesus said to them, "Don't your Scriptures say, 'I said, "You are gods"'? The Scriptures cannot be discredited. So if God calls people gods (and they are the people to whom he gave the Scriptures), why do you say that I'm dishonoring God because I said, 'I'm the Son of God'? God set me apart for this holy purpose and has sent me into the world. If I'm not doing the things my Father does, don't believe me. But if I'm doing those things and you refuse to believe me, then at least believe the things that I'm doing. Then you will know and recognize that the Father is in me and that I am in the Father."

The Jews tried to arrest Jesus again, but he got away from them. He went back across the Jordan River and stayed in the place where John first baptized people.

Many people went to Jesus. They said, "John didn't perform any miracles, but everything John said about this man is true." Many people there believed in Jesus.

THE NARROW DOOR
(LUKE 13:22–30)

Then Jesus traveled and taught in one city and village after another on his way to Jerusalem.

Someone asked him, "Sir, are only a few people going to be saved?"

He answered, "Try hard to enter through the narrow door. I can guarantee that many will try to enter, but they won't succeed. After the homeowner gets up and closes the door, it's too late. You can stand outside, knock at the door, and say, 'Sir, open the door for us!' But he will answer you, 'I don't know who you are.' Then you will say, 'We ate and drank with you, and you taught in our streets.' But he will tell you, 'I don't know who you are. Get away from me, all you evil people.' Then you will cry and be in extreme pain. That's what you'll do when you see Abraham, Isaac, Jacob, and all the prophets. They'll be in the kingdom of God, but you'll be thrown out. People will come from all over the world and will eat in the kingdom of God. Some who are last will be first, and some who are first will be last."

The Narrow Door

When Jesus spoke of the narrow door, he was referring to the result of man's choice to be disobedient. There simply is no room for people to live in accordance with the social and cultural norms of this world while also expecting to be able to gain entry into the kingdom of God. The Bible is clear that there are two paths to choose from in life—wisdom or folly; life or death; Jesus or not Jesus. Because we have chosen to sin, the way to true life becomes narrower and narrower, harder and harder to perceive and enter into. Jesus wasn't trying to exclude people; he was simply affirming what most have already chosen—a way of life that leads to death.

JESUS WARNS JERUSALEM
(LUKE 13:31–35)

At that time some Pharisees told Jesus, "Get out of here, and go somewhere else! Herod wants to kill you."

Jesus said to them, "Tell that fox that I will force demons out of people and heal people today and tomorrow. I will finish my work on the third day. But I must be on my way today, tomorrow, and the next day. It's not possible for a prophet to die outside Jerusalem.

"Jerusalem, Jerusalem, you kill the prophets and stone to death those sent to you! How often I wanted to gather your children together the way a hen gathers her chicks under her wings! But you were not willing! Your house will be abandoned. I can guarantee that you will not see me again until you say, 'Blessed is the one who comes in the name of the Lord!'"

JESUS ATTENDS A BANQUET
(LUKE 14:1–24)

On a day of worship Jesus went to eat at the home of a prominent Pharisee. The guests were watching Jesus very closely.

A man whose body was swollen with fluid was there. Jesus reacted by asking the Pharisees and the experts in Moses' Teachings, "Is it right to heal on the day of worship or not?" But they didn't say a thing.

So Jesus took hold of the man, healed him, and sent him away. Jesus asked them, "If your son or your ox falls into a well on a day of worship, wouldn't you pull him out immediately?" They couldn't argue with him about this.

Then Jesus noticed how the guests always chose the places of honor. So he used this illustration when he spoke to them: "When someone invites you to a wedding, don't take the place of honor. Maybe someone more important than you was invited. Then your host would say to you, 'Give this person your place.' Embarrassed, you would have to take the place of least honor. So when you're invited, take the place of least honor. Then, when your host comes, he will tell you, 'Friend, move to a more honorable place.' Then all the other guests will see how you are honored. Those who honor themselves will be humbled, but people who humble themselves will be honored."

Then he told the man who had invited him, "When you invite people for lunch or dinner, don't invite only your friends, family, other relatives, or rich neighbors. Otherwise, they will return the favor. Instead, when you give a banquet, invite the poor, the handicapped, the lame, and the blind. Then you will be blessed because they don't have any way to pay you back. You will be paid back when those who have God's approval come back to life."

One of those eating with him heard this. So he said to Jesus, "The person who will be at the banquet in the kingdom of God is blessed."

Jesus said to him, "A man gave a large banquet and invited many people. When it was time for the banquet, he sent his servant to tell those who were invited, 'Come! Everything is ready now.'

"Everyone asked to be excused. The first said to him, 'I bought a field, and I need to see it. Please excuse me.' Another said, 'I bought five pairs of oxen, and I'm on my way to see how well they plow. Please excuse me.' Still another said, 'I recently got married, and that's why I can't come.'

"The servant went back to report this to his master. Then the master of the house became angry. He told his servant, 'Run to every street and alley in the city! Bring back the poor, the handicapped, the blind, and the lame.'

"The servant said, 'Sir, what you've ordered has been done. But there is still room for more people.'

"Then the master told his servant, 'Go to the roads and paths! Urge the people to come to my house. I want it to be full. I can guarantee that none of those invited earlier will taste any food at my banquet.'"

THE COST OF BEING A DISCIPLE
(LUKE 14:25–35)

Large crowds were traveling with Jesus. He turned to them and said, "If people come to me and are not ready to abandon their fathers, mothers, wives, children, brothers, and sisters, as well as their own lives, they cannot be my disciples. So those who do not carry their crosses and follow me cannot be my disciples.

"Suppose you want to build a tower. You would first sit down and figure out what it costs. Then you would see if you have enough money to finish it. Otherwise, if you lay a foundation and can't finish the building, everyone who watches will make fun of you. They'll say, 'This person started to build but couldn't finish the job.'

"Or suppose a king is going to war against another king. He would first sit down and think things through. Can he and his 10,000 soldiers fight against a king with 20,000 soldiers? If he can't, he'll send ambassadors to ask for terms of peace while the other king is still far away. In the same way, none of you can be my disciples unless you give up everything.

"Salt is good. But if salt loses its taste, how will you restore its flavor? It's not any good for the ground or for the manure pile. People throw it away.

"Let the person who has ears listen!"

Price of Discipleship

Many have noted that the lack of depth among some new believers stems from the fact that they have not really given up their old way of life. Many have simply tacked Jesus on top. Yet, Jesus calls his followers to a deeper level of commitment that costs them *everything*. Becoming a follower of Christ is an all-or-nothing venture. There is no room for halfhearted commitment. At this point in his ministry the disciples probably did not fully understand Jesus' reference to carrying a cross, but later on, this saying would take on special significance, symbolizing both their need to associate with Jesus in life and in death as well as the willingness to give up everything they had in order to follow Jesus.

THE LOST SHEEP, THE LOST COIN, THE LOST SON
(LUKE 15:1–32) *~see also Matthew 18:12–14~*

All the tax collectors and sinners came to listen to Jesus. But the Pharisees and the scribes complained, "This man welcomes sinners and eats with them."

Jesus spoke to them using this illustration: "Suppose a man has 100 sheep and loses one of them. Doesn't he leave the 99 sheep grazing in the pasture and look for the lost sheep until he finds it? When he finds it, he's happy. He puts that sheep on his shoulders and goes home. Then he calls his friends and neighbors together and says to them, 'Let's celebrate! I've found my lost sheep!' I can guarantee that there will be more happiness in heaven over one person who turns to God and changes the way he thinks and acts than over 99 people who already have turned to God and have his approval."

"Suppose a woman has ten coins and loses one. Doesn't she light a lamp, sweep the house, and look for the coin carefully until she finds it? When she finds it, she calls her friends and neighbors together and says, 'Let's celebrate! I've found the coin that I lost.' So I can guarantee that God's angels are happy about one person who turns to God and changes the way he thinks and acts."

Then Jesus said, "A man had two sons. The younger son said to his father, 'Father, give me my share of the property.' So the father divided his property between his two sons.

"After a few days, the younger son gathered his possessions and left for a country far away from home. There he wasted everything he had on a wild lifestyle. He had nothing left when a severe famine spread throughout that country. He had nothing to live on. So he got a job from someone in that country and was sent to feed pigs in the fields. No one in the country would give him any food, and he was so hungry that he would have eaten what the pigs were eating.

"Finally, he came to his senses. He said, 'How many of my father's hired men have more food than they can eat, while I'm starving to death here? I'll go at once to my father, and I'll say to him, "Father, I've sinned against heaven and you. I don't deserve to be called your son anymore. Make me one of your hired men."'

"So he went at once to his father. While he was still at a distance, his father saw him and felt sorry for him. He ran to his son, put his arms around him, and kissed him. Then his son said to him, 'Father, I've sinned against heaven and you. I don't deserve to be called your son anymore.'

"The father said to his servants, 'Hurry! Bring out the best robe, and put it on him. Put a ring on his finger and sandals on his feet. Bring the fattened calf, kill it, and let's celebrate with a feast. My son was dead and has come back to life. He was lost but has been found.' Then they began to celebrate.

"His older son was in the field. As he was coming back to the house, he heard music and dancing. He called to one of the servants and asked what was happening.

"The servant told him, 'Your brother has come home. So your father has killed the fattened calf to celebrate your brother's safe return.'

"Then the older son became angry and wouldn't go into the house. His father came out and begged him to come in. But he answered his father, 'All these years I've worked like a slave for you. I've never disobeyed one of your commands. Yet, you've never given me so much as a little goat for a celebration with my friends. But this son of yours spent your money on prostitutes, and when he came home, you killed the fattened calf for him.'

"His father said to him, 'My child, you're always with me. Everything I have is yours. But we have something to celebrate, something to be happy about. This brother of yours was dead but has come back to life. He was lost but has been found.'"

JESUS SPEAKS ABOUT DISHONESTY
(LUKE 16:1–18)

Then Jesus said to his disciples, "A rich man had a business manager. The manager was accused of wasting the rich man's property. So the rich man called for his manager and said to him, 'What's this I hear about you? Let me examine your books. It's obvious that you can't manage my property any longer.'

"The manager thought, 'What should I do? My master is taking my job away from me. I'm not strong enough to dig, and I'm ashamed to beg. I know what I'll do so that people will welcome me into their homes when I've lost my job.'

"So the manager called for each one of his master's debtors. He said to the first, 'How much do you owe my master?'

"The debtor replied, 'Eight hundred gallons of olive oil.'

"The manager told him, 'Take my master's ledger. Quick! Sit down, and write "four hundred!"'

"Then he asked another debtor, 'How much do you owe?'

"The debtor replied, 'A thousand bushels of wheat.'

"The manager told him, 'Take the ledger, and write "eight hundred!"'

"The master praised the dishonest manager for being so clever. Worldly people are more clever than spiritually-minded people when it comes to dealing with others."

Jesus continued, "I'm telling you that although wealth is often used in dishonest ways, you should use it to make friends for yourselves. When life is over, you will be welcomed into an eternal home. Whoever can be trusted with very little can also be trusted with a lot. Whoever is dishonest with very little is dishonest with a lot. Therefore, if you can't be trusted with wealth that is often used dishonestly, who will trust you with wealth that is real? If you can't be trusted with someone else's wealth, who will give you your own?

"A servant cannot serve two masters. He will hate the first master and love the second, or he will be devoted to the first and despise the second. You cannot serve God and wealth."

The Pharisees, who love money, heard all this and were making sarcastic remarks about him. So Jesus said to them, "You try to justify your actions in front of people. But God knows what's in your hearts. What is important to humans is disgusting to God.

"Moses' Teachings and the Prophets were in force until the time of John. Since that time, people have been telling the Good News about the kingdom of God, and everyone is trying to force their way into it. It is easier for the earth and the heavens to disappear than to drop a comma from Moses' Teachings.

"Any man who divorces his wife to marry another woman is committing adultery. The man who marries a woman divorced in this way is committing adultery."

A RICH MAN AND LAZARUS
(LUKE 16:19–31)

"There was a rich man who wore expensive clothes. Every day was like a party to him. There was also a beggar named Lazarus who was regularly brought to the gate of the rich man's house. Lazarus would have eaten any scraps that fell from the rich man's table. Lazarus was covered with sores, and dogs would lick them.

"One day the beggar died, and the angels carried him to be with Abraham. The rich man also died and was buried. He went to hell, where he was constantly tortured. As he looked up, in the distance he saw Abraham and Lazarus. He yelled, 'Father Abraham! Have mercy on me! Send Lazarus to dip the tip of his finger in water to cool off my tongue. I am suffering in this fire.'

"Abraham replied, 'Remember, my child, that you had a life filled with good times, while Lazarus' life was filled with misery. Now he has peace here, while you suffer. Besides, a wide area separates us. People couldn't cross it in either direction even if they wanted to.'

"The rich man responded, 'Then I ask you, Father, to send Lazarus back to my father's home. I have five brothers. He can warn them so that they won't end up in this place of torture.'

"Abraham replied, 'They have Moses' Teachings and the Prophets. Your brothers should listen to them!'

"The rich man replied, 'No, Father Abraham! If someone comes back to them from the dead, they will turn to God and change the way they think and act.'

"Abraham answered him, 'If they won't listen to Moses' Teachings and the Prophets, they won't be persuaded even if someone comes back to life.'"

The Rich Man and Lazarus

The contrast between the rich man and Lazarus once again recalls the stern admonitions of the Old Testament prophets regarding Israel's and Judah's failure to care for the poor and needy. In failing to show compassion they made it clear that they lacked the same desire for justice that God held so dear. Jesus makes it clear through this parable that this life is the only one we have control over. Whatever we may profess with our mouths, ultimately our actions show who we really are, and there is no possibility for repentance after death. It is telling that Abraham, the father of the Jewish people, condemns the rich man and his family for possessing "Moses' Teachings and the Prophets" yet failing to do anything with them. The warning should have sent a chill down the back of any Pharisee or religious leader who considered himself to be morally perfect but who nevertheless failed to fully grasp the complete picture of what God expected.

ISSUES OF FAITH
(LUKE 17:1–10) ~see also Matthew 18:6–10; Mark 9:42–50~

Jesus told his disciples, "Situations that cause people to lose their faith are certain to arise. But how horrible it will be for the person who causes someone to lose his faith! It would be best for that person to be thrown into the sea with a large stone hung around his neck than for him to cause one of these little ones to lose his faith. So watch yourselves!

"If a believer sins, correct him. If he changes the way he thinks and acts, forgive him. Even if he wrongs you seven times in one day and comes back to you seven times and says that he is sorry, forgive him."

Then the apostles said to the Lord, "Give us more faith."

The Lord said, "If you have faith the size of a mustard seed, you could say to this mulberry tree, 'Pull yourself up by the roots, and plant yourself in the sea!' and it would obey you.

"Suppose someone has a servant who is plowing fields or watching sheep. Does he tell his servant when he comes from the field, 'Have something to eat'? No. Instead, he tells his servant, 'Get dinner ready for me! After you serve me my dinner, you can eat yours.' He doesn't thank the servant for following orders. That's the way it is with you. When you've done everything you're ordered to do, say, 'We're worthless servants. We've only done our duty.'"

JESUS RAISES LAZARUS AND TALKS ABOUT THE FUTURE

One of the most significant miracles Jesus performed was raising Lazarus from the dead. Since it occurred in a location so close to Jerusalem, the news spread rapidly, enraging the religious leaders even further. As the end of his life drew nearer, Jesus continued to use every available opportunity to explain to his disciples what was about to happen—preaching to them both about his death and resurrection and also about his ultimate return to bring judgment. In the meantime Jesus continued his healing ministry and brought about radical change in a tax collector of diminutive stature. This section closes with the powerful moment when Mary anoints Jesus with a bottle of perfume, presaging his coming death and burial.

JESUS BRINGS LAZARUS BACK TO LIFE
(JOHN 11:1–44)

Lazarus, who lived in Bethany, the village where Mary and her sister Martha lived, was sick. (Mary was the woman who poured perfume on the Lord and wiped his feet with her hair. Her brother Lazarus was the one who was sick.)

So the sisters sent a messenger to tell Jesus, "Lord, your close friend is sick."

When Jesus heard the message, he said, "His sickness won't result in death. Instead, this sickness will bring glory to God so that the Son of God will receive glory through it."

Jesus loved Martha, her sister, and Lazarus. Yet, when Jesus heard that Lazarus was sick, he stayed where he was for two more days.

Then, after the two days, Jesus said to his disciples, "Let's go back to Judea."

The disciples said to him, "Rabbi, not long ago the Jews wanted to stone you to death. Do you really want to go back there?"

Jesus answered, "Aren't there twelve hours of daylight? Those who walk during the day don't stumble, because they see the light of this world. However, those who walk at night stumble because they have no light in themselves."

After Jesus said this, he told his disciples, "Our friend Lazarus is sleeping, and I'm going to Bethany to wake him."

His disciples said to him, "Lord, if he's sleeping, he'll get well."

Jesus meant that Lazarus was dead, but the disciples thought Jesus meant that Lazarus was only sleeping. Then Jesus told them plainly, "Lazarus has died, but I'm glad that I wasn't there so that you can grow in faith. Let's go to Lazarus."

Thomas, who was called Didymus, said to the rest of the disciples, "Let's go so that we, too, can die with Jesus."

When Jesus arrived, he found that Lazarus had been in the tomb for four days. (Bethany was near Jerusalem, not quite two miles away.) Many Jews had come to Martha and Mary to comfort them about their brother.

When Martha heard that Jesus was coming, she went to meet him. Mary stayed at home. Martha told Jesus, "Lord, if you had been here, my brother would not have died. But even now I know that God will give you whatever you ask him."

Jesus told Martha, "Your brother will come back to life."

Martha answered Jesus, "I know that he'll come back to life on the last day, when everyone will come back to life."

Jesus said to her, "I am the one who brings people back to life, and I am life itself. Those who believe in me will live even if they die. Everyone who lives and believes in me will never die. Do you believe that?"

Martha said to him, "Yes, Lord, I believe that you are the Messiah, the Son of God, the one who was expected to come into the world."

After Martha had said this, she went back home and whispered to her sister Mary, "The teacher is here, and he is calling for you."

When Mary heard this, she got up quickly and went to Jesus. (Jesus had not yet come into the village but was still where Martha had met him.) The Jews who were comforting Mary in the house saw her get up quickly and leave. So they followed her. They thought that she was going to the tomb to cry. When Mary arrived where Jesus was and saw him, she knelt at his feet and said, "Lord, if you had been here, my brother would not have died."

When Jesus saw her crying, and the Jews who were crying with her, he was deeply moved and troubled.

So Jesus asked, "Where did you put Lazarus?"

They answered him, "Lord, come and see."

Jesus cried. The Jews said, "See how much Jesus loved him." But some of the Jews asked, "Couldn't this man who gave a blind man sight keep Lazarus from dying?"

Deeply moved again, Jesus went to the tomb. It was a cave with a stone covering the entrance. Jesus said, "Take the stone away."

Martha, the dead man's sister, told Jesus, "Lord, there must already be a stench. He's been dead for four days."

Jesus said to her, "Didn't I tell you that if you believe, you would see God's glory?" So the stone was moved away from the entrance of the tomb.

Jesus looked up and said, "Father, I thank you for hearing me. I've known that you always hear me. However, I've said this so that the crowd standing around me will believe that you sent me." After Jesus had said this, he shouted as loudly as he could, "Lazarus, come out!"

The dead man came out. Strips of cloth were wound around his feet and hands, and his face was wrapped with a handkerchief. Jesus told them, "Free Lazarus, and let him go."

The Raising of Lazarus

Jesus had previously raised two other people from the dead (the son of a widow from Nain, Luke 7:11–17, and the daughter of the religious leader Jairus, Mark 5:21–43). However, something significant happened with Lazarus that made this miracle different. From the point of view of narrative plot, this is the last major miracle given in the Gospel of John before the action moves to the Passion Week. Moreover, as the next reading makes clear, this miracle was the tipping point that caused the Jewish leaders to put in place a plan to kill Jesus. However, for all those gathered, this was an extremely public declaration of Jesus' divine power over death itself, a miracle that presaged his own coming death and resurrection.

THE JEWISH COUNCIL PLANS TO KILL JESUS
(JOHN 11:45–57)

Many Jews who had visited Mary and had seen what Jesus had done believed in him. But some of them went to the Pharisees and told them what Jesus had done. So the chief priests and the Pharisees called a meeting of the council. They asked, "What are we doing? This man is performing a lot of miracles. If we let him continue what he's doing, everyone will believe in him. Then the Romans will take away our position and our nation."

One of them, Caiaphas, who was chief priest that year, told them, "You people don't know anything. You haven't even considered this: It is better for one man to die for the people than for the whole nation to be destroyed."

Caiaphas didn't say this on his own. As chief priest that year, he prophesied that Jesus would die for the Jewish nation. He prophesied that Jesus wouldn't die merely for this nation, but that Jesus would die to bring God's scattered children together and make them one.

From that day on, the Jewish council planned to kill Jesus. So Jesus no longer walked openly among the Jews. Instead, he left Bethany and went to the countryside near the desert, to a city called Ephraim, where he stayed with his disciples.

The Jewish Passover was near. Many people came from the countryside to Jerusalem to purify themselves before the Passover. As they stood in the temple courtyard, they looked for Jesus and asked each other, "Do you think that he'll avoid coming to the festival?" (The chief priests and the Pharisees had given orders that whoever knew where Jesus was should tell them so that they could arrest him.)

TEN MEN WITH A SKIN DISEASE ARE HEALED
(LUKE 17:11–19)

Jesus traveled along the border between Samaria and Galilee on his way to Jerusalem. As he went into a village, ten men with a skin disease met him. They stood at a distance and shouted, "Jesus, Teacher, have mercy on us!"

When he saw them, he told them, "Show yourselves to the priests." As they went, they were made clean. When one of them saw that he was healed, he turned back and praised God in a loud voice. He quickly bowed at Jesus' feet and thanked him. (The man was a Samaritan.)

Jesus asked, "Weren't ten men made clean? Where are the other nine? Only this foreigner came back to praise God."

Jesus told the man, "Get up, and go home! Your faith has made you well."

JESUS TEACHES ABOUT THE TIME WHEN HE WILL COME AGAIN
(LUKE 17:20–37)

The Pharisees asked Jesus when the kingdom of God would come.

He answered them, "People can't observe the coming of the kingdom of God. They can't say, 'Here it is!' or 'There it is!' You see, the kingdom of God is within you."

Jesus said to his disciples, "The time will come when you will long to see one of the days of the Son of Man, but you will not see it. People will say, 'There he is!' or 'Here he is!' Don't run after those people. The day of the Son of Man will be like lightning that flashes from one end of the sky to the other. But first he must suffer a lot and be rejected by the people of his day.

"When the Son of Man comes again, the situation will be like the time of Noah. People were eating, drinking, and getting married until the day that Noah went into the ship. Then the flood destroyed all of them.

"The situation will also be like the time of Lot. People were eating, drinking, buying and selling, planting and building. But on the day that Lot left Sodom, fire and sulfur rained from the sky and destroyed all of them. The day when the Son of Man is revealed will be like that.

"On that day those who are on the roof shouldn't come down to get their belongings out of their houses. Those who are in the field shouldn't turn back. Remember Lot's wife! Those who try to save their lives will lose them, and those who lose their lives will save them.

"I can guarantee that on that night if two people are in one bed, one will be taken and the other one will be left. Two women will be grinding grain together. One will be taken, and the other one will be left."

They asked him, "Where, Lord?"

Jesus told them, "Vultures will gather wherever there is a dead body."

The Day of the Lord

Our world is fractured and not at all the way it was supposed to be. With Adam and Eve's fateful decision to eat the fruit, sin entered the world, and since then everything has been corrupted as a result. The good news, shared repeatedly throughout the Old Testament, especially by the prophets, is that God loves us too much to let it all go to waste. His plan of redemption and restoration has begun in the life, death, and resurrection of Jesus Christ, and will be completed when Christ returns in the final judgment. The prophets looked forward eagerly to the day of the Lord, when all would be made right. That "day" was set in motion by Jesus but awaits complete fulfillment when he returns.

TWO PARABLES ABOUT PRAYER
(LUKE 18:1–14)

Jesus used this illustration with his disciples to show them that they need to pray all the time and never give up. He said, "In a city there was a judge who didn't fear God or respect people. In that city there was also a widow who kept coming to him and saying, 'Give me justice.'

"For a while the judge refused to do anything. But then he thought, 'This widow really annoys me. Although I don't fear God or respect people, I'll have to give her justice. Otherwise, she'll keep coming to me until she wears me out.'"

The Lord added, "Pay attention to what the dishonest judge thought. Won't God give his chosen people justice when they cry out to him for help day and night? Is he slow to help them? I can guarantee that he will give them justice quickly. But when the Son of Man comes, will he find faith on earth?"

Jesus also used this illustration with some who were sure that God approved of them while they looked down on everyone else. He said, "Two men went into the temple courtyard to pray. One was a Pharisee, and the other was a tax collector. The Pharisee stood up and prayed, 'God, I thank you that I'm not like other people! I'm not a robber or a dishonest person. I haven't committed adultery. I'm not even like this tax collector. I fast twice a week, and I give you a tenth of my entire income.'

"But the tax collector was standing at a distance. He wouldn't even look up to heaven. Instead, he became very upset, and he said, 'God, be merciful to me, a sinner!'

"I can guarantee that this tax collector went home with God's approval, but the Pharisee didn't. Everyone who honors himself will be humbled, but the person who humbles himself will be honored."

A DISCUSSION ABOUT DIVORCE AND CELIBACY
(MATTHEW 19:1–12) ~see also Mark 10:1–12~

When Jesus finished speaking, he left Galilee and traveled along the other side of the Jordan River to the territory of Judea. Large crowds followed him, and he healed them there.

Some Pharisees came to test him. They asked, "Can a man divorce his wife for any reason?"

Jesus answered, "Haven't you read that the Creator made them male and female in the beginning and that he said, 'That's why a man will leave his father and mother and will remain united with his wife, and the two will be one'? So they are no longer two but one. Therefore, don't let anyone separate what God has joined together."

The Pharisees asked him, "Why, then, did Moses order a man to give his wife a written notice to divorce her?"

Jesus answered them, "Moses allowed you to divorce your wives because you're heartless. It was never this way in the beginning. I can guarantee that whoever divorces his wife for any reason other than her unfaithfulness is committing adultery if he marries another woman."

The disciples said to him, "If that is the only reason a man can use to divorce his wife, it's better not to get married."

He answered them, "Not everyone can do what you suggest. Only those who have that gift can. For example, some men are celibate because they were born that way. Others are celibate because they were castrated. Still others have decided to be celibate because of the kingdom of heaven. If anyone can do what you've suggested, then he should do it."

Marriage and Divorce

At issue here was a debate between two "schools" of the Pharisees. One group favored the interpretations and teaching of Rabbi Hillel. The other group followed Rabbi Shammai. The two schools held opposing views regarding divorce, and in this section Jesus is challenged to pick a side. Craig Blomberg, professor of New Testament at Denver Seminary, explains that Rabbi Hillel tended to be a bit more liberal in his interpretations of the law, in this case arguing for a reading of Deuteronomy 24:1 that allowed divorce for any reason at all. Rabbi Shammai, in contrast, preferred a reading that allowed divorce only in the case of infidelity. From this passage and Jesus' comments in Matthew 5:31–32, it is clear that Jesus' ideal is for one man to marry one woman and for no one to be divorced (Beale and Carson, *Commentary on the New Testament Use of the Old Testament*, 23–24).

JESUS BLESSES CHILDREN
(MARK 10:13–16) ~see also Matthew 19:13–15; Luke 18:15–17~

Some people brought little children to Jesus to have him hold them. But the disciples told the people not to do that.

When Jesus saw this, he became irritated. He told them, "Don't stop the children from coming to me. Children like these are part of the kingdom of God. I can guarantee this truth: Whoever doesn't receive the kingdom of God as a little child receives it will never enter it."

Jesus put his arms around the children and blessed them by placing his hands on them.

ETERNAL LIFE IN THE KINGDOM
(MARK 10:17–31) *~see also Matthew 19:16–30; Luke 18:18–30~*

As Jesus was coming out to the road, a man came running to him and knelt in front of him. He asked Jesus, "Good Teacher, what should I do to inherit eternal life?"

Jesus said to him, "Why do you call me good? No one is good except God alone. You know the commandments: Never murder. Never commit adultery. Never steal. Never give false testimony. Never cheat. Honor your father and mother."

The man replied, "Teacher, I've obeyed all these commandments since I was a boy."

Jesus looked at him and loved him. He told him, "You're still missing one thing. Sell everything you have. Give the money to the poor, and you will have treasure in heaven. Then follow me!"

When the man heard that, he looked unhappy and went away sad, because he owned a lot of property.

Jesus looked around and said to his disciples, "How hard it will be for rich people to enter the kingdom of God!"

The disciples were stunned by his words. But Jesus said to them again, "Children, how hard it is to enter the kingdom of God! It is easier for a camel to go through the eye of a needle than for a rich person to enter the kingdom of God."

This amazed his disciples more than ever. They asked each other, "Who, then, can be saved?"

Jesus looked at them and said, "It's impossible for people to save themselves, but it's not impossible for God to save them. Everything is possible for God."

Then Peter spoke up, "We've given up everything to follow you."

Jesus said, "I can guarantee this truth: Anyone who gave up his home, brothers, sisters, mother, father, children, or fields because of me and the Good News will certainly receive a hundred times as much here in this life. They will certainly receive homes, brothers, sisters, mothers, children and fields, along with persecutions. But in the world to come they will receive eternal life. But many who are first will be last, and the last will be first."

What Jesus Really Wants

As in so many places throughout the Bible, the key for understanding a passage is examining the overall context in which it is placed. Jesus' comment was directed specifically at this rich young man, issued as a challenge to his sense of pride in his moral behavior. By pushing this issue of material possessions Jesus showed that the man was not really ready to follow Jesus at all. Jesus thoroughly affirms the importance of the Law as central to all of life. As he says in Matthew 5:17, he came to fulfill the Law, not abolish it. Yet, at the same time Jesus pushes would-be followers to go beyond the Law to find fulfillment, meaning, purpose, and direction in him.

A STORY ABOUT VINEYARD WORKERS (MATTHEW 20:1–16)

"The kingdom of heaven is like a landowner who went out at daybreak to hire workers for his vineyard. After agreeing to pay the workers the usual day's wages, he sent them to work in his vineyard. About 9 a.m. he saw others standing in the marketplace without work. He said to them, 'Work in my vineyard, and I'll give you whatever is right.' So they went.

"He went out again about noon and 3 p.m. and did the same thing. About 5 p.m. he went out and found some others standing around. He said to them, 'Why are you standing here all day long without work?'

"'No one has hired us,' they answered him.

"He said to them, 'Work in my vineyard.'

"When evening came, the owner of the vineyard told the supervisor, 'Call the workers, and give them their wages. Start with the last, and end with the first.'

"Those who started working about 5 p.m. came, and each received a day's wages. When those who had been hired first came, they expected to receive more. But each of them received a day's wages. Although they took it, they began to protest to the owner. They said, 'These last workers have worked only one hour. Yet, you've treated us all the same, even though we worked hard all day under a blazing sun.'

"The owner said to one of them, 'Friend, I'm not treating you unfairly. Didn't you agree with me on a day's wages? Take your money and go! I want to give this last worker as much as I gave you. Can't I do what I want with my own money? Or do you resent my generosity towards others?'

"In this way the last will be first, and the first will be last."

JESUS FORETELLS A THIRD TIME THAT HE WILL DIE AND COME BACK TO LIFE
(MARK 10:32–34) ~see also Matthew 20:17–19; Luke 18:31–34~

Jesus and his disciples were on their way to Jerusalem. Jesus was walking ahead of them. His disciples were shocked that he was going to Jerusalem. The others who followed were afraid. Once again he took the twelve apostles aside. He began to tell them what was going to happen to him. "We're going to Jerusalem. There the Son of Man will be betrayed to the chief priests and the scribes. They will condemn him to death and hand him over to foreigners. They will make fun of him, spit on him, whip him, and kill him. But after three days he will come back to life."

JAMES AND JOHN MAKE A REQUEST
(MARK 10:35–45) ~see also Matthew 20:20–28~

James and John, sons of Zebedee, went to Jesus. They said to him, "Teacher, we want you to do us a favor."

"What do you want me to do for you?" he asked them.

They said to him, "Let one of us sit at your right and the other at your left in your glory."

Jesus said, "You don't realize what you're asking. Can you drink the cup that I'm going to drink? Can you be baptized with the baptism that I'm going to receive?"

"We can," they told him.

Jesus told them, "You will drink the cup that I'm going to drink. You will be baptized with the baptism that I'm going to receive. But I don't have the authority to grant you a seat at my right or left. Those positions have already been prepared for certain people."

When the other ten apostles heard about it, they were irritated with James and John. Jesus called the apostles and said, "You know that the acknowledged rulers of nations have absolute power over people and their officials have absolute authority over people. But that's not the way it's going to be among you. Whoever wants to become great among you will be your servant. Whoever wants to be most important among you will be a slave for everyone. It's the same way with the Son of Man. He didn't come so that others could serve him. He came to serve and to give his life as a ransom for many people."

JESUS GIVES SIGHT TO BARTIMAEUS

(MARK 10:46–52) ~see also *Matthew 20:29–34; Luke 18:35–43*~

Then they came to Jericho. As Jesus, his disciples, and many people were leaving Jericho, a blind beggar named Bartimaeus, son of Timaeus, was sitting by the road. When he heard that Jesus from Nazareth was passing by, he began to shout, "Jesus, Son of David, have mercy on me!"

The people told him to be quiet. But he shouted even louder, "Son of David, have mercy on me!"

Jesus stopped and said, "Call him!" They called the blind man and told him, "Cheer up! Get up! He's calling you." The blind man threw off his coat, jumped up, and went to Jesus.

Jesus asked him, "What do you want me to do for you?"

The blind man said, "Teacher, I want to see again."

Jesus told him, "Go, your faith has made you well."

At once he could see again, and he followed Jesus on the road.

ZACCHAEUS MEETS JESUS

(LUKE 19:1–10)

Jesus was passing through Jericho. A man named Zacchaeus was there. He was the director of tax collectors, and he was rich. He tried to see who Jesus was. But Zacchaeus was a small man, and he couldn't see Jesus because of the crowd. So Zacchaeus ran ahead and climbed a fig tree to see Jesus, who was coming that way.

When Jesus came to the tree, he looked up and said, "Zacchaeus, come down! I must stay at your house today."

Zacchaeus came down and was glad to welcome Jesus into his home. But the people who saw this began to express disapproval. They said, "He went to be the guest of a sinner."

Later, at dinner, Zacchaeus stood up and said to the Lord, "Lord, I'll give half of my property to the poor. I'll pay four times as much as I owe to those I have cheated in any way."

Then Jesus said to Zacchaeus, "You and your family have been saved today. You've shown that you, too, are one of Abraham's descendants. Indeed, the Son of Man has come to seek and to save people who are lost."

Zacchaeus's Amazing Transformation

Tax collectors were widely disliked among the people, since they were known to collect commissions and taxes above and beyond what was owed to the Roman government. In the Gospels tax collectors are frequently associated with sinners and prostitutes. Zacchaeus was called a director of tax collectors, meaning that he was responsible for a group of tax collectors who worked underneath him, and he quite possibly took a cut of their income as well. Without a doubt he was extremely rich, but when he realized who Jesus was he responded quickly, offering to repay all that he had cheated and swindled away from the people four times over. Perhaps the most astonishing note is Jesus' comment that, as a result, this tax collector of tax collectors could now be named as one of Abraham's descendants—a member of the chosen people of God. This claim was probably more shocking to the people gathered in the house than Zacchaeus's promise to give back all he owed.

A STORY ABOUT A KING
(LUKE 19:11–27)

Jesus was getting closer to Jerusalem, and the people thought that the kingdom of God would appear suddenly. While Jesus had the people's attention, he used this illustration. He said, "A prince went to a distant country to be appointed king, and then he returned. Before he left, he called ten of his servants and gave them ten coins. He said to his servants, 'Invest this money until I come back.'

"The citizens of his own country hated him. They sent representatives to follow him and say to the person who was going to appoint him, 'We don't want this man to be our king.'

"After he was appointed king, he came back. Then he said, 'Call those servants to whom I gave money. I want to know how much each one has made by investing.'

"The first servant said, 'Sir, the coin you gave me has earned ten times as much.'

"The king said to him, 'Good job! You're a good servant. You proved that you could be trusted with a little money. Take charge of ten cities.'

"The second servant said, 'The coin you gave me, sir, has made five times as much.'

"The king said to this servant, 'You take charge of five cities.'

"Then the other servant said, 'Sir, look! Here's your coin. I've kept it in a cloth for safekeeping because I was afraid of you. You're a tough person to get along with. You take what isn't yours and harvest grain you haven't planted.'

"The king said to him, 'I'll judge you by what you've said, you evil servant! You knew that I was a tough person to get along with. You knew that I take what isn't mine and harvest grain I haven't planted. Then why didn't you put my money in the bank? When I came back, I could have collected it with interest.' The king told his men, 'Take his coin away, and give it to the man who has ten.'

"They replied, 'Sir, he already has ten coins.'

"'I can guarantee that everyone who has something will be given more. But everything will be taken away from those who don't have much. Bring my enemies, who didn't want me to be their king. Kill them in front of me.'"

MARY PREPARES JESUS' BODY FOR THE TOMB
(JOHN 12:1–11) ~see also Matthew 26:6–13; Mark 14:3–9~

Six days before Passover, Jesus arrived in Bethany. Lazarus, whom Jesus had brought back to life, lived there. Dinner was prepared for Jesus in Bethany. Martha served the dinner, and Lazarus was one of the people eating with Jesus.

Mary took a bottle of very expensive perfume made from pure nard and poured it on Jesus' feet. Then she dried his feet with her hair. The fragrance of the perfume filled the house.

One of his disciples, Judas Iscariot, who was going to betray him, asked, "Why wasn't this perfume sold for a high price and the money given to the poor?" (Judas didn't say this because he cared about the poor but because he was a thief. He was in charge of the moneybag and carried the contributions.) Jesus said to Judas, "Leave her alone! She has done this to prepare me for the day I will be placed in a tomb. You will always have the poor with you, but you will not always have me with you."

A large crowd of Jews found out that Jesus was in Bethany. So they went there not only to see Jesus but also to see Lazarus, whom Jesus had brought back to life. The chief priests planned to kill Lazarus too. Lazarus was the reason why many people were leaving the Jews and believing in Jesus.

section twenty-three

JESUS' FINAL WEEK

Jesus' final week begins on an incredibly high note. The people are excited, enthralled by this man they can't quite figure out. They hailed him as a king, offering worship, waving palm branches, and singing praises. Yet, almost immediately the tone changes. As Jesus engages in direct confrontation with the religious leaders his teaching becomes more strident, and a specific plot brews whereby the leaders plan to kill him. Judas is lured into their scheme and agrees to betray his leader for thirty silver

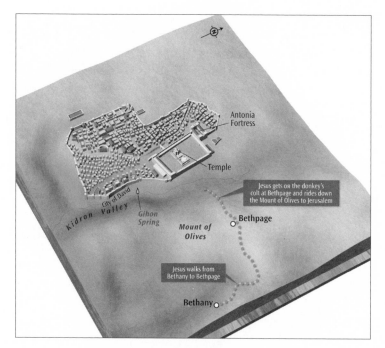

Triumphal Entry

coins. Yet, for those who have ears to hear, his stories reveal that he will return one day and at that time his true followers will receive blessing, while his opponents will be judged.

THE KING COMES TO JERUSALEM
(MATTHEW 21:1–11) ~see also Mark 11:1–11; Luke 19:29–44; John 12:12–19~

When they came near Jerusalem and had reached Bethphage on the Mount of Olives, Jesus sent two disciples ahead of him. He said to them, "Go into the village ahead of you. You will find a donkey tied there and a colt with it. Untie them, and bring them to me. If anyone says anything to you, tell him that the Lord needs them. That person will send them at once."

This happened so that what the prophet had said came true:

"Tell the people of Zion,
'Your king is coming to you.
He's gentle,
riding on a donkey,
on a colt, a young pack animal.'"

The disciples did as Jesus had directed them. They brought the donkey and the colt and put their coats on them for Jesus to sit on. Most of the people spread their coats on the road. Others cut branches from the trees and spread them on the road. The crowd that went ahead of him and that followed him was shouting,

"Hosanna to the Son of David!
Blessed is the one who comes in the name of the Lord!
Hosanna in the highest heaven!"

When Jesus came into Jerusalem, the whole city was in an uproar. People were asking, "Who is this?"

The crowd answered, "This is the prophet Jesus from Nazareth in Galilee."

JESUS THROWS OUT THE MONEYCHANGERS
(MATTHEW 21:12–17) ~see also Mark 11:15–19; Luke 19:45–48~

Jesus went into the temple courtyard and threw out everyone who was buying and selling there. He overturned the moneychangers' tables and the chairs of those who sold pigeons. He told them, "Scripture says, 'My house will be called a house of prayer,' but you're turning it into a gathering place for thieves!"

Blind and lame people came to him in the temple courtyard, and he healed them.

When the chief priests and the scribes saw the amazing miracles he performed and the children shouting in the temple courtyard, "Hosanna to the Son of David!" they were irritated. They said to him, "Do you hear what these children are saying?"

Jesus replied, "Yes, I do. Have you never read, 'From the mouths of little children and infants, you have created praise'?"

He left them and went out of the city to Bethany and spent the night there.

SOME GREEKS ASK TO SEE JESUS
(JOHN 12:20–50)

Some Greeks were among those who came to worship during the Passover festival. They went to Philip (who was from Bethsaida in Galilee) and told him, "Sir, we would like to meet Jesus." Philip told Andrew, and they told Jesus.

Jesus replied to them, "The time has come for the Son of Man to be glorified. I can guarantee this truth: A single grain of wheat doesn't produce anything unless it is planted in the ground and dies. If it dies, it will produce a lot of grain.

Those who love their lives will destroy them, and those who hate their lives in this world will guard them for everlasting life. Those who serve me must follow me. My servants will be with me wherever I will be. If people serve me, the Father will honor them.

"I am too deeply troubled now to know how to express my feelings. Should I say, 'Father, save me from this time of suffering'? No! I came for this time of suffering. Father, give glory to your name."

A voice from heaven said, "I have given it glory, and I will give it glory again."

The crowd standing there heard the voice and said that it had thundered. Others in the crowd said that an angel had talked to him. Jesus replied, "That voice wasn't for my benefit but for yours.

"This world is being judged now. The ruler of this world will be thrown out now. When I have been lifted up from the earth, I will draw all people toward me." By saying this, he indicated how he was going to die.

The crowd responded to him, "We have heard from the Scriptures that the Messiah will remain here forever. So how can you say, 'The Son of Man must be lifted up from the earth'? Who is this 'Son of Man'?"

Jesus answered the crowd, "The light will still be with you for a little while. Walk while you have light so that darkness won't defeat you. Those who walk in the dark don't know where they're going. While you have the light, believe in the light so that you will become people whose lives show the light."

After Jesus had said this, he was concealed as he left. Although they had seen Jesus perform so many miracles, they wouldn't believe in him. In this way the words of the prophet Isaiah came true:

> "Lord, who has believed our message?
> To whom has the Lord's power been revealed?"

So the people couldn't believe because, as Isaiah also said,

> "God blinded them
> and made them close-minded
> so that their eyes don't see
> and their minds don't understand.
> And they never turn to me for healing!"

Isaiah said this because he had seen Jesus' glory and had spoken about him.

Many rulers believed in Jesus. However, they wouldn't admit it publicly because the Pharisees would have thrown them out of the synagogue. They were more concerned about what people thought of them than about what God thought of them.

Then Jesus said loudly, "Whoever believes in me believes not only in me but also in the one who sent me. Whoever sees me sees the one who sent me. I am the light that has come into the world so that everyone who believes in me will not live in the dark. If anyone hears my words and doesn't follow them, I don't condemn them. I didn't come to condemn the world but to save the world. Those who reject me by not accepting what I say have a judge appointed for them. The words that I have spoken will judge them on the last day. I have not spoken on my own. Instead, the Father who sent me told me what I should say and how I should say it. I know that what he commands is eternal life. Whatever I say is what the Father told me to say."

JESUS CURSES THE FIG TREE
(MATTHEW 21:18–22) ~see also Mark 11:12–14, 20–25~

In the morning, as Jesus returned to the city, he became hungry. When he saw a fig tree by the road, he went up to the tree and found nothing on it but leaves. He said to the tree, "May fruit never grow on you again!" At once the fig tree dried up.

The disciples were surprised to see this. They asked, "How did the fig tree dry up so quickly?"

Jesus answered them, "I can guarantee this truth: If you have faith and do not doubt, you will be able to do what I did to the fig tree. You could also say to this mountain, 'Be uprooted and thrown into the sea,' and it will happen. Have faith that you will receive whatever you ask for in prayer."

JESUS' AUTHORITY CHALLENGED
(MATTHEW 21:23–46) ~see also Mark 11:27–12:12; Luke 20:1–19~

Then Jesus went into the temple courtyard and began to teach. The chief priests and the leaders of the people came to him. They asked, "What gives you the right to do these things? Who told you that you could do this?"

Jesus answered them, "I, too, have a question for you. If you answer it for me, I'll tell you why I have the right to do these things. Did John's right to baptize come from heaven or from humans?"

They discussed this among themselves. They said, "If we say, 'from heaven,' he will ask us, 'Then why didn't you believe him?' But if we say, 'from humans,' we're afraid of what the crowd might do. All those people think of John as a prophet." So they answered Jesus, "We don't know."

Jesus told them, "Then I won't tell you why I have the right to do these things.

"What do you think about this? A man had two sons. He went to the first and said, 'Son, go to work in the vineyard today.'

"His son replied, 'I don't want to!' But later he changed his mind and went.

"The father went to the other son and told him the same thing. He replied, 'I will, sir,' but he didn't go.

"Which of the two sons did what the father wanted?"

"The first," they answered.

Jesus said to them, "I can guarantee this truth: Tax collectors and prostitutes are going into the kingdom of God ahead of you. John came to you and showed you the way that God wants you to live, but you didn't believe him. The tax collectors and prostitutes believed him. But even after you had seen that, you didn't change your minds and believe him.

"Listen to another illustration. A landowner planted a vineyard. He put a wall around it, made a winepress, and built a watchtower. Then he leased it to vineyard workers and went on a trip.

"When the grapes were getting ripe, he sent his servants to the workers to collect his share of the produce. The workers took his servants and beat one, killed another, and stoned a third to death. So the landowner sent more servants. But the workers treated them the same way.

"Finally, he sent his son to them. He thought, 'They will respect my son.'

"When the workers saw his son, they said to one another, 'This is the heir. Let's kill him and get his inheritance.' So they grabbed him, threw him out of the vineyard, and killed him.

"Now, when the owner of the vineyard comes, what will he do to those workers?"

They answered, "He will destroy those evil people. Then he will lease the vineyard to other workers who will give him his share of the produce when it is ready."

Jesus asked them, "Have you never read in the Scriptures:

'The stone that the builders rejected
    has become the cornerstone.
The Lord is responsible for this,
    and it is amazing for us to see'?

That is why I can guarantee that the kingdom of God will be taken away from you and given to a people who will produce what God wants. Anyone who falls on this stone will be broken. If the stone falls on anyone, it will crush that person."

When the chief priests and the Pharisees heard his illustrations, they knew that he was talking about them. They wanted to arrest him but were afraid of the crowds, who thought he was a prophet.

Reversed Expectations

The most telling part of this passage comes at the end, when Matthew notes that the chief priests and the Pharisees knew that Jesus was using these parables to talk about them. Although many parables and stories were hard to understand, in this case the religious leaders saw all too clearly what Jesus was trying to say. In the story of the landowner and the vineyard, Jesus is the son and heir of the vineyard, while the servants sent beforehand represent the prophets. Any listener would have to conclude that the landowner, when he returns, has every right to punish his workers. Running like a thread through these stories is the theme of an inheritance being removed from one party and given to another, of expectations being reversed.

A STORY ABOUT A WEDDING RECEPTION
(MATTHEW 22:1–14)

Again Jesus used stories as illustrations when he spoke to them. He said, "The kingdom of heaven is like a king who planned a wedding for his son. He sent his servants to those who had been invited to the wedding, but they refused to come. He sent other servants to tell the people who had been invited, 'I've prepared dinner. My bulls and fattened calves have been butchered. Everything is ready. Come to the wedding!'

"But they paid no attention and went away. Some went to work in their own fields, and others went to their businesses. The rest grabbed the king's servants, mistreated them, and then killed them.

"The king became angry. He sent his soldiers, killed those murderers, and burned their city.

"Then the king said to his servants, 'The wedding is ready, but those who were invited don't deserve the honor. Go where the roads leave the city. Invite everyone you find to the wedding.' The servants went into the streets and brought in all the good people and all the evil people they found. And the wedding hall was filled with guests.

"When the king came to see the guests, he saw a person who was not dressed in the wedding clothes provided for the guests. He said to him, 'Friend, how did you get in here without proper wedding clothes?'

"The man had nothing to say. Then the king told his servants, 'Tie his hands and feet, and throw him outside into the darkness. People will cry and be in extreme pain there.'

"Therefore, many are invited, but few of those are chosen to stay."

RELIGIOUS LEADERS QUESTION JESUS
(MATTHEW 22:15–46) ~see also Mark 12:13–37a; Luke 20:20–44~

Then the Pharisees went away and planned to trap Jesus into saying the wrong thing. They sent their disciples to him along with Herod's followers. They said to him, "Teacher, we know that you tell the truth and that you teach the truth about the way of God. You don't favor individuals because of who they are. So tell us what you think. Is it right to pay taxes to the emperor or not?"

Jesus recognized their evil plan, so he asked, "Why do you test me, you hypocrites? Show me a coin used to pay taxes."

They brought him a coin. He said to them, "Whose face and name is this?"

They replied, "The emperor's."

Then he said to them, "Very well, give the emperor what belongs to the emperor, and give God what belongs to God."

They were surprised to hear this. Then they left him alone and went away.

On that day some Sadducees, who say that people will never come back to life, came to Jesus. They asked him, "Teacher, Moses said, 'If a man dies childless, his brother should marry his widow and have children for his brother.' There were seven brothers among us. The first married and died. Since he had no children, he left his widow to his brother. The second brother also died, as well as the third, and the rest of the seven brothers. At last the woman died. Now, when the dead come back to life, whose wife will she be? All seven brothers had been married to her."

Jesus answered, "You're mistaken because you don't know the Scriptures or God's power. When people come back to life, they don't marry. Rather, they are like the angels in heaven. Haven't you read what God told you about the dead coming back to life? He said, 'I am the God of Abraham, Isaac, and Jacob.' He's not the God of the dead but of the living."

He amazed the crowds who heard his teaching.

LOVE GOD AND YOUR NEIGHBOR
(MATTHEW 22:34–40) ~see also Mark 12:28–34~

When the Pharisees heard that Jesus had silenced the Sadducees, they gathered together. One of them, an expert in Moses' Teachings, tested Jesus by asking, "Teacher, which commandment is the greatest in Moses' Teachings?"

Jesus answered him, "'Love the Lord your God with all your heart, with all your soul, and with all your mind.' This is the greatest and most important commandment. The second is like it: 'Love your neighbor as you love yourself.' All of Moses' Teachings and the Prophets depend on these two commandments."

While the Pharisees were still gathered, Jesus asked them, "What do you think about the Messiah? Whose son is he?"

They answered him, "David's."

He said to them, "Then how can David, guided by the Spirit, call him Lord? David says,

> 'The Lord said to my Lord,
>> "Take the highest position in heaven
>>> until I put your enemies under your control."'

If David calls him Lord, how can he be his son?"

No one could answer him, and from that time on no one dared to ask him another question.

THE HYPOCRISY OF THE SCRIBES AND THE PHARISEES
(MATTHEW 23:1–39) ~see also Mark 12:37b–40; Luke 20:45–47~

Then Jesus said to the crowds and to his disciples, "The scribes and the Pharisees teach with Moses' authority. So be careful to do everything they tell you. But don't follow their example, because they don't practice what they preach. They make loads that are hard to carry and lay them on the shoulders of the people. However, they are not willing to lift a finger to move them.

"They do everything to attract people's attention. They make their headbands large and the tassels on their shawls long. They love the place of honor at dinners and the front seats in synagogues. They love to be greeted in the marketplaces and to have people call them Rabbi. But don't make others call you Rabbi, because you have only one teacher, and you are all followers. And don't call anyone on earth your father, because you have only one Father, and he is in heaven. Don't make others call you a leader, because you have only one leader, the Messiah. The person who is greatest among you will be your servant. Whoever honors himself will be humbled, and whoever humbles himself will be honored.

"How horrible it will be for you, scribes and Pharisees! You hypocrites! You lock people out of the kingdom of heaven. You don't enter it yourselves, and you don't permit others to enter when they try. [Some manuscripts add: "How horrible it will be for you, scribes and Pharisees! You hypocrites! You rob widows by taking their houses and then say long prayers to make yourselves look good. You will receive a most severe punishment."]

"How horrible it will be for you, scribes and Pharisees! You hypocrites! You cross land and sea to recruit a single follower, and when you do, you make that person twice as fit for hell as you are.

"How horrible it will be for you, you blind guides! You say, 'To swear an oath by the temple doesn't mean a thing. But to swear an oath by the gold in the temple means a person must keep his oath.' You blind fools! What is more important, the gold or the temple that made the gold holy? Again you say, 'To swear an oath by the altar doesn't mean a thing. But to swear an oath by the gift on the altar means a person must keep his oath.' You blind men! What is more important, the gift or the altar that makes the gift holy? To swear an oath by the altar is to swear by it and by everything on it. To swear an oath by the temple is to swear by it and by the one who lives there. And to swear an oath by heaven is to swear by God's throne and the one who sits on it.

"How horrible it will be for you, scribes and Pharisees! You hypocrites! You give God one-tenth of your mint, dill, and cumin. But you have neglected justice, mercy, and faithfulness. These are the most important things in Moses' Teachings. You should have done these things without neglecting the others. You blind guides! You strain gnats out of your wine, but you swallow camels.

"How horrible it will be for you, scribes and Pharisees! You hypocrites! You clean the outside of cups and dishes. But inside they are full of greed and uncontrolled desires. You blind Pharisees! First clean the inside of the cups and dishes so that the outside may also be clean.

"How horrible it will be for you, scribes and Pharisees! You hypocrites! You are like whitewashed graves that look beautiful on the outside but inside are full of dead people's bones and every kind of impurity. So on the outside you look as though you have God's approval, but inside you are full of hypocrisy and lawlessness.

"How horrible it will be for you, scribes and Pharisees! You hypocrites! You build tombs for the prophets and decorate the monuments of those who had

God's approval. Then you say, 'If we had lived at the time of our ancestors, we would not have helped to murder the prophets.' So you testify against yourselves that you are the descendants of those who murdered the prophets. Go ahead, finish what your ancestors started!

"You snakes! You poisonous snakes! How can you escape being condemned to hell? I'm sending you prophets, wise men, and teachers of the Scriptures. You will kill and crucify some of them. Others you will whip in your synagogues and persecute from city to city. As a result, you will be held accountable for all the innocent blood of those murdered on earth, from the murder of righteous Abel to that of Zechariah, son of Barachiah, whom you murdered between the temple and the altar. I can guarantee this truth: The people living now will be held accountable for all these things.

"Jerusalem, Jerusalem, you kill the prophets and stone to death those sent to you! How often I wanted to gather your children together the way a hen gathers her chicks under her wings! But you were not willing! Your house will be abandoned, deserted. I can guarantee that you will not see me again until you say, 'Blessed is the one who comes in the name of the Lord!'"

Condemning Religious Hypocrisy

This scathing rebuke from Jesus is shocking in its unequivocal condemnation of the scribes and Pharisees. Jesus is clear that for all their external religiosity and pious behavior, inside, their hearts are completely corrupt. As the religious leaders of the people, the ones who should be guarding God's honor, they were responsible for living and acting differently. Interestingly, Jesus does not condemn their behavior but rather condemns the attitude of their hearts. The Law is not to be ignored or dismissed, but Jesus is calling on all people to live lives that are congruent with the beliefs they claim to hold.

A WIDOW'S CONTRIBUTION
(LUKE 21:1–4) ~see also Mark 12:41–44~

Looking up, Jesus saw people, especially the rich, dropping their gifts into the temple offering box. He noticed a poor widow drop in two small coins. He said, "I can guarantee this truth: This poor widow has given more than all the others. All of these people have given what they could spare. But she, in her poverty, has given everything she had to live on."

JESUS TEACHES HIS DISCIPLES ON THE MOUNT OF OLIVES
(MATTHEW 24:1–35) ~see also Mark 13:1–31; Luke 21:5–33~

As Jesus left the temple courtyard and was walking away, his disciples came to him. They proudly pointed out to him the temple buildings. Jesus said to them, "You see all these buildings, don't you? I can guarantee this truth: Not one of these stones will be left on top of another. Each one will be torn down."

As Jesus was sitting on the Mount of Olives, his disciples came to him privately and said, "Tell us, when will this happen? What will be the sign that you are coming again, and when will the world come to an end?"

Jesus answered them, "Be careful not to let anyone deceive you. Many will come using my name. They will say, 'I am the Messiah,' and they will deceive many people.

"You will hear of wars and rumors of wars. Don't be alarmed! These things must happen, but they don't mean that the end has come. Nation will fight against nation and kingdom against kingdom. There will be famines and earthquakes in various places. All of these are only the beginning pains of the end.

"Then they will hand you over to those who will torture and kill you. All nations will hate you because you are committed to me. Then many will lose faith. They will betray and hate each other. Many false prophets will appear and deceive many people. And because there will be more and more lawlessness, most people's love will grow cold. But the person who endures to the end will be saved.

"This Good News about the kingdom will be spread throughout the world as a testimony to all nations. Then the end will come.

"The prophet Daniel said that the disgusting thing that will cause destruction will stand in the holy place. When you see this (let the reader take note), those of you in Judea should flee to the mountains. Those who are on the roof should not come down to get anything out of their houses. Those who are in the field should not turn back to get their coats.

"How horrible it will be for the women who are pregnant or who are nursing babies in those days. Pray that it will not be winter or a day of worship when you flee. There will be a lot of misery at that time, a kind of misery that has not happened from the beginning of the world until now and will certainly never happen again. If God does not reduce the number of those days, no one will be saved. But those days will be reduced because of those whom God has chosen.

"At that time don't believe anyone who tells you, 'Here is the Messiah!' or 'There he is!' False messiahs and false prophets will appear. They will work spectacular, miraculous signs and do wonderful things to deceive, if possible, even those whom God has chosen. Listen! I've told you this before it happens. So if someone tells you, 'He's in the desert!' don't go out looking for him. And don't believe anyone who says, 'He's in a secret place!' The Son of Man will come again just as lightning flashes from east to west. Vultures will gather wherever there is a dead body.

"Immediately after the misery of those days, the sun will turn dark, the moon will not give light, the stars will fall from the sky, and the powers of the universe will be shaken.

"Then the sign of the Son of Man will appear in the sky. All the people on earth will cry in agony when they see the Son of Man coming on the clouds in the sky with power and great glory. He will send out his angels with a loud trumpet call, and from every direction under the sky, they will gather those whom God has chosen.

"Learn from the story of the fig tree. When its branch becomes tender and it sprouts leaves, you know that summer is near. In the same way, when you see all these things, you know that he is near, at the door.

"I can guarantee this truth: This generation will not disappear until all these things take place. The earth and the heavens will disappear, but my words will never disappear."

NO ONE KNOWS WHEN THE SON OF MAN WILL RETURN
(MATTHEW 24:36–51)

"No one knows when that day or hour will come. Even the angels in heaven and the Son don't know. Only the Father knows.

"When the Son of Man comes again, it will be exactly like the days of Noah. In the days before the flood, people were eating, drinking, and getting married until the day that Noah went into the ship. They were not aware of what was happening until the flood came and swept all of them away. That is how it will be when the Son of Man comes again.

"At that time two men will be working in the field. One will be taken, and the other one will be left. Two women will be working at a mill. One will be taken, and the other one will be left.

"Therefore, be alert, because you don't know on what day your Lord will return. You realize that if a homeowner had known at what time of the night a thief was coming, he would have stayed awake. He would not have let the thief break into his house. Therefore, you, too, must be ready because the Son of Man will return when you least expect him.

"Who, then, is the faithful and wise servant? The master will put that person in charge of giving the other servants their food at the right time. That servant will be blessed if his master finds him doing this job when he comes. I can guarantee this truth: He will put that servant in charge of all his property. On the other hand, that servant, if he is wicked, may think that it will be a long time before his master comes. The servant may begin to beat the other servants and eat and drink with the drunks. His master will return unexpectedly. Then his master will severely punish him and assign him a place with the hypocrites. People will cry and be in extreme pain there."

A STORY ABOUT TEN BRIDESMAIDS
(MATTHEW 25:1–13)

"When the end comes, the kingdom of heaven will be like ten bridesmaids. They took their oil lamps and went to meet the groom. Five of them were foolish, and five were wise. The foolish bridesmaids took their lamps, but they didn't take any extra oil. The wise bridesmaids, however, took along extra oil for their lamps. Since the groom was late, all the bridesmaids became drowsy and fell asleep.

"At midnight someone shouted, 'The groom is here! Come to meet him!' Then all the bridesmaids woke up and got their lamps ready.

"The foolish ones said to the wise ones, 'Give us some of your oil. Our lamps are going out.'

"But the wise bridesmaids replied, 'We can't do that. There won't be enough for both of us. Go! Find someone to sell you some oil.'

"While they were buying oil, the groom arrived. The bridesmaids who were ready went with him into the wedding hall, and the door was shut.

"Later the other bridesmaids arrived and said, 'Sir, sir, open the door for us!'

"But he answered them, 'I don't even know who you are!'

"So stay awake, because you don't know the day or the hour."

Preparing for Jesus' Return

Jesus tells the people to get ready for the day when the kingdom of heaven will arrive, but what does that mean in practical terms? God frequently presents himself as the groom waiting for his bride and here Jesus uses that same imagery to great effect. While he doesn't give specifics regarding preparation, he does place a strong emphasis on being ready for his return. The point is made in stark contrast to the complacency and hypocrisy of the religious leaders, who were content to live as if God was not about to return. Preparation from Jesus' point of view must have included a heart that wholeheartedly embraced his mission and vision for the world, eagerly serving him throughout this life, without letting anything get in the way.

A STORY ABOUT THREE SERVANTS
(MATTHEW 25:14–30)

"The kingdom of heaven is like a man going on a trip. He called his servants and entrusted some money to them. He gave one man ten thousand dollars, another four thousand dollars, and another two thousand dollars. Each was given money based on his ability. Then the man went on his trip.

"The one who received ten thousand dollars invested the money at once and doubled his money. The one who had four thousand dollars did the same and also doubled his money. But the one who received two thousand dollars went off, dug a hole in the ground, and hid his master's money.

"After a long time the master of those servants returned and settled accounts with them. The one who received ten thousand dollars brought the additional ten thousand. He said, 'Sir, you gave me ten thousand dollars. I've doubled the amount.'

"His master replied, 'Good job! You're a good and faithful servant! You proved that you could be trusted with a small amount. I will put you in charge of a large amount. Come and share your master's happiness.'

"The one who received four thousand dollars came and said, 'Sir, you gave me four thousand dollars. I've doubled the amount.'

"His master replied, 'Good job! You're a good and faithful servant! You proved that you could be trusted with a small amount. I will put you in charge of a large amount. Come and share your master's happiness.'

"Then the one who received two thousand dollars came and said, 'Sir, I knew that you are a hard person to please. You harvest where you haven't planted and gather where you haven't scattered any seeds. I was afraid. So I hid your two thousand dollars in the ground. Here's your money!'

"His master responded, 'You evil and lazy servant! If you knew that I harvest where I haven't planted and gather where I haven't scattered, then you should have invested my money with the bankers. When I returned, I would have received my money back with interest. Take the two thousand dollars away from him! Give it to the one who has the ten thousand! To all who have, more will be given, and they will have more than enough. But everything will be taken away from those who don't have much. Throw this useless servant outside into the darkness. People will cry and be in extreme pain there.'"

JESUS WILL JUDGE THE WORLD
(MATTHEW 25:31–46)

"When the Son of Man comes in his glory and all his angels are with him, he will sit on his glorious throne. The people of every nation will be gathered in front of him. He will separate them as a shepherd separates the sheep from the goats. He will put the sheep on his right but the goats on his left.

"Then the king will say to those on his right, 'Come, my Father has blessed you! Inherit the kingdom prepared for you from the creation of the world. I was hungry, and you gave me something to eat. I was thirsty, and you gave me something to drink. I was a stranger, and you took me into your home. I needed clothes, and you gave me something to wear. I was sick, and you took care of me. I was in prison, and you visited me.'

"Then the people who have God's approval will reply to him, 'Lord, when did we see you hungry and feed you or see you thirsty and give you something to drink? When did we see you as a stranger and take you into our homes or see you in need of clothes and give you something to wear? When did we see you sick or in prison and visit you?'

"The king will answer them, 'I can guarantee this truth: Whatever you did for one of my brothers or sisters, no matter how unimportant they seemed, you did for me.'

"Then the king will say to those on his left, 'Get away from me! God has cursed you! Go into everlasting fire that was prepared for the devil and his angels! I was hungry, and you gave me nothing to eat. I was thirsty, and you gave me nothing to drink. I was a stranger, and you didn't take me into your homes. I needed clothes, and you didn't give me anything to wear. I was sick and in prison, and you didn't take care of me.'

"They, too, will ask, 'Lord, when did we see you hungry or thirsty or as a stranger or in need of clothes or sick or in prison and didn't help you?'

"He will answer them, 'I can guarantee this truth: Whatever you failed to do for one of my brothers or sisters, no matter how unimportant they seemed, you failed to do for me.'

"These people will go away into eternal punishment, but those with God's approval will go into eternal life."

THE PLOT TO KILL JESUS
(MATTHEW 26:1–5) ~see also Mark 14:1–2; Luke 22:1–6~

When Jesus finished saying all these things, he told his disciples, "You know that the Passover will take place in two days. At that time the Son of Man will be handed over to be crucified."

Then the chief priests and the leaders of the people gathered in the palace of the chief priest Caiaphas. They made plans to arrest Jesus in an underhanded way and to kill him. But they said, "We shouldn't arrest him during the festival, or else there may be a riot among the people."

JUDAS PLANS TO BETRAY JESUS
(MATTHEW 26:14–16) ~see also Mark 14:10–11; Luke 22:3–6~

Then one of the twelve apostles, the one named Judas Iscariot, went to the chief priests. He asked, "What will you pay me if I hand him over to you?"

They offered him 30 silver coins. From then on, he looked for a chance to betray Jesus.

JESUS' LAST SUPPER WITH HIS DISCIPLES

Jesus' last few hours with his disciples are revealed to us in extensive detail. From the Last Supper to the washing of the feet and the prediction of Peter's denial, this was such a significant event that the Gospel writers included as much as possible in their accounts. While accounts of healings and ministry activity move quickly, the narrative slows down significantly

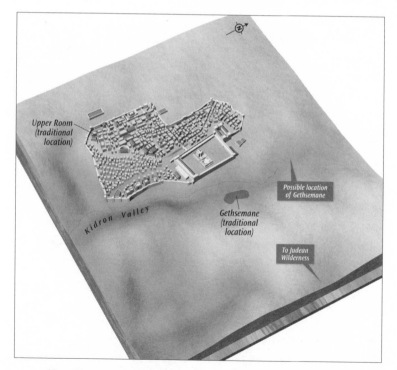

New Testament Jerusalem and the Garden of Gethsemane

as we read lengthy explanations of the coming Holy Spirit, the importance of remaining connected to the "true vine," and the incredible prayer in John 17 as Jesus prays for himself, his disciples, and the church that would be formed after his departure. It is a powerful model for us that Jesus spent the last hours and minutes before his arrest in intense prayer with his heavenly Father.

THE PASSOVER
(LUKE 22:7–20) ~see also Matthew 26:17–20, 26–30; Mark 14:12–17, 22–26~

The day came during the Festival of Unleavened Bread when the Passover lamb had to be killed. Jesus sent Peter and John and told them, "Go, prepare the Passover lamb for us to eat."

They asked him, "Where do you want us to prepare it?"

He told them, "Go into the city, and you will meet a man carrying a jug of water. Follow him into the house he enters. Tell the owner of the house that the teacher asks, 'Where is the room where I can eat the Passover meal with my disciples?' He will take you upstairs and show you a large furnished room. Get things ready there."

The disciples left. They found everything as Jesus had told them and prepared the Passover.

When it was time to eat the Passover meal, Jesus and the apostles were at the table. Jesus said to them, "I've had a deep desire to eat this Passover with you before I suffer. I can guarantee that I won't eat it again until it finds its fulfillment in the kingdom of God." Then he took a cup and spoke a prayer of thanksgiving. He said, "Take this, and share it. I can guarantee that from now on I won't drink this wine until the kingdom of God comes."

Then Jesus took bread and spoke a prayer of thanksgiving. He broke the bread, gave it to them, and said, "This is my body, which is given up for you. Do this to remember me."

When supper was over, he did the same with the cup. He said, "This cup that is poured out for you is the new promise made with my blood."

The Passover

The Passover and the Festival of Unleavened Bread were celebrations of events surrounding Israel's escape from Egypt—the exodus. After nine horrible plagues sent on Egypt, Pharaoh still refused to let the people go, so God sent a final sign—killing the firstborn of every house. However, he passed over the houses of the Israelites who had sprinkled their doorposts with the blood of a lamb. During this same time the Israelites were to remove all yeast from their house in preparation for a quick escape. The symbolism is powerful—as the Passover lamb was slain to protect the Israelites from death, so Jesus, too, was slain to save the world from the punishment for sin—death.

JESUS WASHES THE DISCIPLES' FEET
(JOHN 13:1–20)

Before the Passover festival, Jesus knew that the time had come for him to leave this world and go back to the Father. Jesus loved his own who were in the world, and he loved them to the end.

While supper was taking place, the devil had already put the idea of betraying Jesus into the mind of Judas, son of Simon Iscariot.

The Father had put everything in Jesus' control. Jesus knew that. He also knew that he had come from God and was going back to God. So he got up from the table, removed his outer clothes, took a towel, and tied it around his waist. Then he poured water into a basin and began to wash the disciples' feet and dry them with the towel that he had tied around his waist.

When Jesus came to Simon Peter, Peter asked him, "Lord, are you going to wash my feet?"

Jesus answered Peter, "You don't know now what I'm doing. You will understand later."

Peter told Jesus, "You will never wash my feet."

Jesus replied to Peter, "If I don't wash you, you don't belong to me."

Simon Peter said to Jesus, "Lord, don't wash only my feet. Wash my hands and my head too!"

Jesus told Peter, "People who have washed are completely clean. They need to have only their feet washed. All of you, except for one, are clean." (Jesus knew who was going to betray him. That's why he said, "All of you, except for one, are clean.")

After Jesus had washed their feet and put on his outer clothes, he took his place at the table again. Then he asked his disciples, "Do you understand what

I've done for you? You call me teacher and Lord, and you're right because that's what I am. So if I, your Lord and teacher, have washed your feet, you must wash each other's feet. I've given you an example that you should follow. I can guarantee this truth: Slaves are not superior to their owners, and messengers are not superior to the people who send them. If you understand all of this, you are blessed whenever you follow my example.

"I'm not talking about all of you. I know the people I've chosen to be apostles. However, I've made my choice so that Scripture will come true. It says, 'The one who eats my bread has turned against me.' I'm telling you now before it happens. Then, when it happens, you will believe that I am the one.

"I can guarantee this truth: Whoever accepts me accepts the one who sent me."

JESUS KNOWS WHO WILL BETRAY HIM
(JOHN 13:21–32) ~see also Matthew 26:21–25; Mark 14:18–21; Luke 22:21–23~

After saying this, Jesus was deeply troubled. He declared, "I can guarantee this truth: One of you is going to betray me!"

The disciples began looking at each other and wondering which one of them Jesus meant.

One disciple, the one whom Jesus loved, was near him at the table. Simon Peter motioned to that disciple and said, "Ask Jesus whom he's talking about!"

Leaning close to Jesus, that disciple asked, "Lord, who is it?"

Jesus answered, "He's the one to whom I will give this piece of bread after I've dipped it in the sauce." So Jesus dipped the bread and gave it to Judas, son of Simon Iscariot.

Then, after Judas took the piece of bread, Satan entered him. So Jesus told him, "Hurry! Do what you have to do." No one at the table knew why Jesus said this to him. Judas had the moneybag. So some thought that Jesus was telling him to buy what they needed for the festival or to give something to the poor.

Judas took the piece of bread and immediately went outside. It was night.

When Judas was gone, Jesus said, "The Son of Man is now glorified, and because of him God is glorified. If God is glorified because of the Son of Man, God will glorify the Son of Man because of himself, and he will glorify the Son of Man at once."

JESUS PREDICTS PETER'S DENIAL
(JOHN 13:33–38) ~see also Matthew 26:31–35; Mark 14:27–31; Luke 22:31–34~

Jesus said, "Dear children, I will still be with you for a little while. I'm telling you what I told the Jews. You will look for me, but you can't go where I'm going.

"I'm giving you a new commandment: Love each other in the same way that I have loved you. Everyone will know that you are my disciples because of your love for each other."

Simon Peter asked him, "Lord, where are you going?"

Jesus answered him, "You can't follow me now to the place where I'm going. However, you will follow me later."

Peter said to Jesus, "Lord, why can't I follow you now? I'll give my life for you."

Jesus replied, "Will you give your life for me? I can guarantee this truth: No rooster will crow until you say three times that you don't know me."

JESUS PROMISES TO SEND THE HOLY SPIRIT
(JOHN 14:1–31)

"Don't be troubled. Believe in God, and believe in me. My Father's house has many rooms. If that were not true, would I have told you that I'm going to prepare a place for you? If I go to prepare a place for you, I will come again. Then I will bring you into my presence so that you will be where I am. You know the way to the place where I am going."

Thomas said to him, "Lord, we don't know where you're going. So how can we know the way?"

Jesus answered him, "I am the way, the truth, and the life. No one goes to the Father except through me. If you have known me, you will also know my Father. From now on you know him through me and have seen him in me."

Philip said to Jesus, "Lord, show us the Father, and that will satisfy us."

Jesus replied, "I have been with all of you for a long time. Don't you know me yet, Philip? The person who has seen me has seen the Father. So how can you say, 'Show us the Father'? Don't you believe that I am in the Father and the Father is in me? What I'm telling you doesn't come from me. The Father, who lives in me, does what he wants. Believe me when I say that I am in the Father and that the Father is in me. Otherwise, believe me because of the things I do.

"I can guarantee this truth: Those who believe in me will do the things that I am doing. They will do even greater things because I am going to the Father. I will do anything you ask the Father in my name so that the Father will be given glory because of the Son. If you ask me to do something, I will do it.

"If you love me, you will obey my commandments. I will ask the Father, and he will give you another helper who will be with you forever. That helper is the Spirit of Truth. The world cannot accept him, because it doesn't see or know him. You know him, because he lives with you and will be in you.

"I will not leave you all alone. I will come back to you. In a little while the world will no longer see me, but you will see me. You will live because I live. On that day you will know that I am in my Father and that you are in me and that I am in you. Whoever knows and obeys my commandments is the person who loves me. Those who love me will have my Father's love, and I, too, will love them and show myself to them."

Judas (not Iscariot) asked Jesus, "Lord, what has happened that you are going to reveal yourself to us and not to the world?"

Jesus answered him, "Those who love me will do what I say. My Father will love them, and we will go to them and make our home with them. A person who doesn't love me doesn't do what I say. I don't make up what you hear me say. What I say comes from the Father who sent me.

"I have told you this while I'm still with you. However, the helper, the Holy Spirit, whom the Father will send in my name, will teach you everything. He will remind you of everything that I have ever told you.

"I'm leaving you peace. I'm giving you my peace. I don't give you the kind of peace that the world gives. So don't be troubled or cowardly. You heard me tell you, 'I'm going away, but I'm coming back to you.' If you loved me, you would be glad that I'm going to the Father, because the Father is greater than I am.

"I'm telling you this now before it happens. When it does happen, you will believe. The ruler of this world has no power over me. But he's coming, so I won't talk with you much longer. However, I want the world to know that I love the Father and that I am doing exactly what the Father has commanded me to do. Get up! We have to leave."

JESUS, THE TRUE VINE
(JOHN 15:1–27)

Then Jesus said, "I am the true vine, and my Father takes care of the vineyard. He removes every one of my branches that doesn't produce fruit. He also prunes every branch that does produce fruit to make it produce more fruit.

"You are already clean because of what I have told you. Live in me, and I will live in you. A branch cannot produce any fruit by itself. It has to stay attached to the vine. In the same way, you cannot produce fruit unless you live in me.

"I am the vine. You are the branches. Those who live in me while I live in them will produce a lot of fruit. But you can't produce anything without me. Whoever doesn't live in me is thrown away like a branch and dries up. Branches like this are gathered, thrown into a fire, and burned. If you live in me and what I say lives in you, then ask for anything you want, and it will be yours. You give glory to my Father when you produce a lot of fruit and therefore show that you are my disciples.

"I have loved you the same way the Father has loved me. So live in my love. If you obey my commandments, you will live in my love. I have obeyed my Father's commandments, and in that way I live in his love. I have told you this so that you will be as joyful as I am, and your joy will be complete. Love each other as I have loved you. This is what I'm commanding you to do. The greatest love you can show is to give your life for your friends. You are my friends if you obey my commandments. I don't call you servants anymore, because a servant doesn't know what his master is doing. But I've called you friends because I've made known to you everything that I've heard from my Father. You didn't choose me, but I chose you. I have appointed you to go, to produce fruit that will last, and to ask the Father in my name to give you whatever you ask for. Love each other. This is what I'm commanding you to do.

"If the world hates you, realize that it hated me before it hated you. If you had anything in common with the world, the world would love you as one of its own. But you don't have anything in common with the world. I chose you from the world, and that's why the world hates you. Remember what I told you: 'A servant isn't greater than his master.' If they persecuted me, they will also persecute you. If they did what I said, they will also do what you say. Indeed, they will do all this to you because you are committed to me, since they don't know the one who sent me. If I hadn't come and spoken to them, they wouldn't have any sin. But now they have no excuse for their sin. The person who hates me also hates my Father. If I hadn't done among them what no one else has done, they wouldn't have any sin. But now they have seen and hated both me and my Father. In this way what is written in their Scriptures has come true: 'They hate me for no reason.'

"The helper whom I will send to you from the Father will come. This helper, the Spirit of Truth who comes from the Father, will declare the truth about me. You will declare the truth, too, because you have been with me from the beginning."

SADNESS WILL TURN TO JOY
(JOHN 16:1–33)

Jesus continued, "I have said these things to you so that you won't lose your faith. You will be thrown out of synagogues. Certainly, the time is coming when people who murder you will think that they are serving God. They will do these things to you because they haven't known the Father or me. But I've told you this so that when it happens you'll remember what I've told you. I didn't tell you this at first, because I was with you.

"Now I'm going to the one who sent me. Yet, none of you asks me where I'm going. But because I've told you this, you're filled with sadness. However, I am telling you the truth: It's good for you that I'm going away. If I don't go away, the helper won't come to you. But if I go, I will send him to you. He will come to convict the world of sin, to show the world what has God's approval, and to convince the world that God judges it. He will convict the world of sin, because people don't believe in me. He will show the world what has God's approval, because I'm going to the Father and you won't see me anymore. He will convince the world that God judges it, because the ruler of this world has been judged.

"I have a lot more to tell you, but that would be too much for you now. When the Spirit of Truth comes, he will guide you into the full truth. He won't speak on his own. He will speak what he hears and will tell you about things to come. He will give me glory, because he will tell you what I say. Everything the Father says is also what I say. That is why I said, 'He will take what I say and tell it to you.'

"In a little while you won't see me anymore. Then in a little while you will see me again."

Some of his disciples said to each other, "What does he mean? He tells us that in a little while we won't see him. Then he tells us that in a little while we will see him again and that he's going to the Father." So they were asking each other, "What does he mean when he says, 'In a little while'? We don't understand what he's talking about."

Jesus knew they wanted to ask him something. So he said to them, "Are you trying to figure out among yourselves what I meant when I said, 'In a little while you won't see me, and in a little while you will see me again'? I can guarantee this truth: You will cry because you are sad, but the world will be happy. You will feel pain, but your pain will turn to happiness. A woman has pain when her time to give birth comes. But after the child is born, she doesn't remember the pain anymore because she's happy that a child has been brought into the world.

"Now you're in a painful situation. But I will see you again. Then you will be happy, and no one will take that happiness away from you. When that day comes, you won't ask me any more questions. I can guarantee this truth: If you ask the Father for anything in my name, he will give it to you. So far you haven't asked for anything in my name. Ask and you will receive so that you can be completely happy.

"I have used examples to illustrate these things. The time is coming when I won't use examples to speak to you. Rather, I will speak to you about the Father in plain words. When that day comes, you will ask for what you want in my name. I'm telling you that I won't have to ask the Father for you. The Father loves you because you have loved me and have believed that I came from God. I left the Father and came into the world. Again, as I've said, I'm going to leave the world and go back to the Father."

His disciples said, "Now you're talking in plain words and not using examples. Now we know that you know everything. You don't need to wait for questions to be asked. Because of this, we believe that you have come from God."

Jesus replied to them, "Now you believe. The time is coming, and is already here, when all of you will be scattered. Each of you will go your own way and leave me all alone. Yet, I'm not all alone, because the Father is with me. I've told you this so that my peace will be with you. In the world you'll have trouble. But cheer up! I have overcome the world."

JESUS PRAYS FOR HIMSELF, HIS DISCIPLES, AND HIS CHURCH
(JOHN 17:1–26)

After saying this, Jesus looked up to heaven and said, "Father, the time is here. Give your Son glory so that your Son can give you glory. After all, you've given him authority over all humanity so that he can give eternal life to all those you gave to him. This is eternal life: to know you, the only true God, and Jesus Christ, whom you sent. On earth I have given you glory by finishing the work you gave me to do. Now, Father, give me glory in your presence with the glory I had with you before the world existed.

"I made your name known to the people you gave me. They are from this world. They belonged to you, and you gave them to me. They did what you told them. Now they know that everything you gave me comes from you, because I gave them the message that you gave me. They have accepted this message, and they know for sure that I came from you. They have believed that you sent me.

"I pray for them. I'm not praying for the world but for those you gave me, because they are yours. Everything I have is yours, and everything you have is mine. I have been given glory by the people you have given me. I won't be in the world much longer, but they are in the world, and I'm coming back to you. Holy Father, keep them safe by the power of your name, the name that you gave me, so that their unity may be like ours. While I was with them, I kept them safe by the power of your name, the name that you gave me. I watched over them, and none of them, except one person, became lost. So Scripture came true.

"But now, Father, I'm coming back to you. I say these things while I'm still in the world so that they will have the same joy that I have. I have given them your message. But the world has hated them because they don't belong to the world any more than I belong to the world. I'm not asking you to take them out of the world but to protect them from the evil one. They don't belong to the world any more than I belong to the world.

"Use the truth to make them holy. Your words are truth. I have sent them into the world the same way you sent me into the world. I'm dedicating myself to this holy work I'm doing for them so that they, too, will use the truth to be holy.

"I'm not praying only for them. I'm also praying for those who will believe in me through their message. I pray that all of these people continue to have unity in the way that you, Father, are in me and I am in you. I pray that they may be united with us so that the world will believe that you have sent me. I have given them the glory that you gave me. I did this so that they are united in the same way we are. I am in them, and you are in me. So they are completely united. In this way the world knows that you have sent me and that you have loved them in the same way you have loved me.

"Father, I want those you have given to me to be with me, to be where I am. I want them to see my glory, which you gave me because you loved me before the world was made. Righteous Father, the world didn't know you. Yet, I knew you, and these disciples have known that you sent me. I have made your name known to them, and I will make it known so that the love you have for me will be in them and I will be in them."

Jesus Prays for His Own

The powerful prayer of Jesus on the night he was betrayed is an almost unbelievable moment in the life and ministry of Jesus. There are no other examples in other religions of God praying on behalf of his people. Yet, here is Jesus, not simply praying for himself but praying for his disciples and also for all "those who will believe." In other words, Jesus included in his prayer all believers throughout history, from the time of his prayer until the present day. That God would go to such lengths to show his love for us is truly incredible. Moreover, it emphasizes here the absolute importance of unity among believers. One of the greatest failures of the Christian church has been the number of divisions created over time among believers in Christ. Jesus' prayer calls us all to a much higher standard.

JESUS PRAYS IN THE GARDEN OF GETHSEMANE
(MATTHEW 26:36–46) ~see also Mark 14:32–42; Luke 22:39–46~

Then Jesus went with the disciples to a place called Gethsemane. He said to them, "Stay here while I go over there and pray."

He took Peter and Zebedee's two sons with him. He was beginning to feel deep anguish. Then he said to them, "My anguish is so great that I feel as if I'm dying. Wait here, and stay awake with me."

After walking a little farther, he quickly bowed with his face to the ground and prayed, "Father, if it's possible, let this cup of suffering be taken away from me. But let your will be done rather than mine."

When he went back to the disciples, he found them asleep. He said to Peter, "Couldn't you stay awake with me for one hour? Stay awake, and pray that you won't be tempted. You want to do what's right, but you're weak."

Then he went away a second time and prayed, "Father, if this cup cannot be taken away unless I drink it, let your will be done."

He found them asleep again because they couldn't keep their eyes open.

After leaving them again, he went away and prayed the same prayer a third time. Then he came back to the disciples and said to them, "You might as well sleep now. The time is near for the Son of Man to be handed over to sinners. Get up! Let's go! The one who is betraying me is near."

JESUS IS ARRESTED AND TRIED BEFORE THE JEWS

When Jesus was arrested, everything seemed to start falling apart. The disciples flee in fear. Peter later returns to catch a glimpse of the trial, but when he is spotted he denies Jesus three times, as Jesus had predicted. The trial is a mockery of justice, illegal in every sense. The religious leaders are unable to generate any significant evidence against him and ultimately it is Jesus who seals his own fate by claiming to be the Messiah, the Son of God. Condemned to death, Jesus is sent off to the Romans. Meanwhile, when

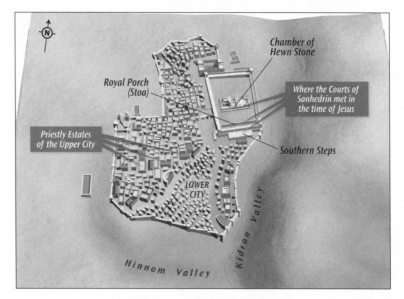

Location of Sanhedrin Courts

Judas realizes what he has done, he returns the money and, in despair, kills himself. From an earthly perspective, the growing ministry of Jesus has collapsed into chaos.

JESUS IS ARRESTED
(JOHN 18:1–11) ~see also Matthew 26:47–56a; Mark 14:43–49; Luke 22:47–53~

After Jesus finished his prayer, he went with his disciples to the other side of the Kidron Valley. They entered the garden that was there.

Judas, who betrayed him, knew the place because Jesus and his disciples often gathered there. So Judas took a troop of soldiers and the guards from the chief priests and Pharisees and went to the garden. They were carrying lanterns, torches, and weapons.

Jesus knew everything that was going to happen to him. So he went to meet them and asked, "Who are you looking for?"

They answered him, "Jesus from Nazareth."

Jesus told them, "I am he."

Judas, who betrayed him, was standing with the crowd. When Jesus told them, "I am he," the crowd backed away and fell to the ground.

Jesus asked them again, "Who are you looking for?"

They said, "Jesus from Nazareth."

Jesus replied, "I told you that I am he. So if you are looking for me, let these other men go." In this way what Jesus had said came true: "I lost none of those you gave me."

Simon Peter had a sword. He drew it, attacked the chief priest's servant, and cut off the servant's right ear. (The servant's name was Malchus.)

Jesus told Peter, "Put your sword away. Shouldn't I drink the cup of suffering that my Father has given me?"

THE DISCIPLES ABANDON JESUS
(MARK 14:50–52) ~see also Matthew 26:56b~

Then all the disciples abandoned him and ran away.

A certain young man was following Jesus. He had nothing on but a linen sheet. They tried to arrest him, but he left the linen sheet behind and ran away naked.

JESUS IS BROUGHT BEFORE ANNAS
(JOHN 18:12–14) ~see also Luke 22:54a~

Then the army officer and the Jewish guards arrested Jesus. They tied Jesus up and took him first to Annas, the father-in-law of Caiaphas. Caiaphas, the chief priest that year, was the person who had advised the Jews that it was better to have one man die for the people.

Who Were Annas and Caiaphas?

Annas had been the high priest from AD 6–15 but his influence remained strong for many years afterwards. As a wealthy and influential figure in Jerusalem, he was still considered high priest, at least in name, long after he had ceased to serve in that role (perhaps in a similar way to American presidents today). He had five sons who also served as high priest, and his son-in-law, Caiaphas, was acting as high priest at the time of the trial of Jesus. The irony of the situation, of course, was that Jesus, the Messiah, was the true High Priest and his initial silence before them was a judgment on the authority of Annas and Caiaphas. As the author of Hebrews would later point out, "Moses' Teachings designated mortals as chief priests even though they had weaknesses. But God's promise, which came after Moses' Teachings, designated the Son who forever accomplished everything that God required" (Heb. 7:28). Jesus did accomplish everything that God required, thereby making the priesthood utterly irrelevant.

THE TRIAL BEFORE THE JEWISH COUNCIL
(MATTHEW 26:57–68) ~see also Mark 14:53–65;
Luke 22:63–71; John 18:19–24~

Those who had arrested Jesus took him to Caiaphas, the chief priest, where the scribes and the leaders had gathered together. Peter followed at a distance until he came to the chief priest's courtyard. He went inside and sat with the guards to see how this would turn out.

The chief priests and the whole council were searching for false testimony to use against Jesus in order to execute him. But they did not find any, although many came forward with false testimony. At last two men came forward. They stated, "This man said, 'I can tear down God's temple and rebuild it in three days.'"

The chief priest stood up and said to Jesus, "Don't you have any answer to what these men testify against you?"

But Jesus was silent.

Then the chief priest said to him, "Swear an oath in front of the living God and tell us, are you the Messiah, the Son of God?"

Jesus answered him, "Yes, I am. But I can guarantee that from now on you will see the Son of Man in the highest position in heaven. He will be coming on the clouds of heaven."

Then the chief priest tore his robes in horror and said, "He has dishonored God! Why do we need any more witnesses? You've just heard him dishonor God! What's your verdict?"

They answered, "He deserves the death penalty!"

Then they spit in his face, hit him with their fists, and some of them slapped him. They said, "You Christ, if you're a prophet, tell us who hit you."

The Jewish Council and Jesus

The Jewish Council, or "Sanhedrin," was a body of religious leaders, perhaps numbering as many as seventy people, who were responsible for handing down decisions on various religious matters. The term was used loosely and could refer both to a full meeting of all members as well as to smaller gatherings of some members. The group was made up of Pharisees, Sadducees, and Scribes, with fairly clear guidelines regarding proper legal procedure. That they were condemning their Messiah was clearly not their intention at all. They were so blinded by their jealousy of his power and following that they could not see Jesus' true identity. Their expectations for what the Messiah would look like were so different that all they could see in Jesus was an impertinent imposter instead of the Son of God.

PETER DENIES JESUS
(LUKE 22:54B–62) ~see also Matthew 26:69–75;
Mark 14:66–72; John 18:15–18, 25–27~

Peter followed at a distance.

Some men had lit a fire in the middle of the courtyard. As they sat together, Peter sat among them. A female servant saw him as he sat facing the glow of the fire. She stared at him and said, "This man was with Jesus."

But Peter denied it by saying, "I don't know him, woman."

A little later someone else saw Peter and said, "You are one of them."

But Peter said, "Not me!"

About an hour later another person insisted, "It's obvious that this man was with him. He's a Galilean!"

But Peter said, "I don't know what you're talking about!"

Just then, while he was still speaking, a rooster crowed. Then the Lord turned and looked directly at Peter. Peter remembered what the Lord had said: "Before a rooster crows today, you will say three times that you don't know me." Then Peter went outside and cried bitterly.

THE JEWISH COUNCIL CONDEMNS JESUS
(MATTHEW 27:1–2)

Early in the morning all the chief priests and the leaders of the people decided to execute Jesus. They tied him up, led him away, and handed him over to Pilate, the governor.

THE DEATH OF JUDAS
(MATTHEW 27:3–10)

Then Judas, who had betrayed Jesus, regretted what had happened when he saw that Jesus was condemned. He brought the 30 silver coins back to the chief priests and leaders. He said, "I've sinned by betraying an innocent man."

They replied, "What do we care? That's your problem."

So he threw the money into the temple, went away, and hanged himself.

The chief priests took the money and said, "It's not right to put it into the temple treasury, because it's blood money." So they decided to use it to buy a potter's field for the burial of strangers. That's why that field has been called the Field of Blood ever since. Then what the prophet Jeremiah had said came true, "They took the 30 silver coins, the price the people of Israel had placed on him, and used the coins to buy a potter's field, as the Lord had directed me."

Consequences for Judas and Peter

Although the difference is subtle in the English translation, the original Greek text draws out the fact that Judas never actually repented of his sin but simply "regretted" it. That is, while his actions caused him to feel regret for what he had done, it was not the kind of godly sorrow that leads to repentance (2 Cor. 7:10). Why this led to his death we can't speculate. Although we know that God struck down Ananias and Sapphira for their sin (Acts 5:1–11) there is no indication of God's direct punishment here. Peter, it would seem, went beyond regret to true sorrow, as indicated by the loving way Jesus treats him when they meet again (John 21).

JESUS IS TRIED BEFORE THE ROMANS

Pilate's mocking question to Jesus, "What is truth?" is a human challenge to God's authority that has echoed down through the millennia, from Adam and Eve's first rebellion all the way to today. In an attempt to wash his hands of the problem, Pilate does everything he can to avoid taking responsibility for the death of a man he knows is innocent. Yet, in pandering to the crowds he ends up releasing a murderer and thief and condemning Jesus to be crucified.

PILATE QUESTIONS JESUS
(JOHN 18:28–38) ~see also Matthew 27:11–14; Mark 15:1–5; Luke 23:1–4~

Early in the morning, Jesus was taken from Caiaphas' house to the governor's palace.

The Jews wouldn't go into the palace. They didn't want to become unclean, since they wanted to eat the Passover. So Pilate came out to them and asked, "What accusation are you making against this man?"

The Jews answered Pilate, "If he weren't a criminal, we wouldn't have handed him over to you."

Pilate told the Jews, "Take him, and try him by your law."

The Jews answered him, "We're not allowed to execute anyone." In this way what Jesus had predicted about how he would die came true.

Pilate went back into the palace, called for Jesus, and asked him, "Are you the king of the Jews?"

Jesus replied, "Did you think of that yourself, or did others tell you about me?"

Pilate answered, "Am I a Jew? Your own people and the chief priests handed you over to me. What have you done?"

Jesus answered, "My kingdom doesn't belong to this world. If my kingdom belonged to this world, my followers would fight to keep me from being handed over to the Jews. My kingdom doesn't have its origin on earth."

Pilate asked him, "So you are a king?"

Jesus replied, "You're correct in saying that I'm a king. I have been born and have come into the world for this reason: to testify to the truth. Everyone who belongs to the truth listens to me."

Pilate said to him, "What is truth?"

After Pilate said this, he went out to the Jews again and told them, "I don't find this man guilty of anything.

PILATE SENDS JESUS TO HEROD
(LUKE 23:6–12)

When Pilate heard that, he asked if the man was from Galilee. When Pilate found out that he was, he sent Jesus to Herod. Herod ruled Galilee and was in Jerusalem at that time.

Herod was very pleased to see Jesus. For a long time he had wanted to see him. He had heard about Jesus and hoped to see him perform some kind of miracle. Herod asked Jesus many questions, but Jesus wouldn't answer him. Meanwhile, the chief priests and the scribes stood there and shouted their accusations against Jesus.

Herod and his soldiers treated Jesus with contempt and made fun of him. They put a colorful robe on him and sent him back to Pilate. So Herod and Pilate became friends that day. They had been enemies before this.

THE CROWD REJECTS JESUS
(MATTHEW 27:15–26) ~see also Mark 15:6–15;
Luke 23:18–25; John 18:39–40~

At every Passover festival the governor would free one prisoner whom the crowd wanted. At that time there was a well-known prisoner by the name of Barabbas. So when the people gathered, Pilate asked them, "Which man do you want me to free for you? Do you want me to free Barabbas or Jesus, who is called Christ?" Pilate knew that they had handed Jesus over to him because they were jealous.

While Pilate was judging the case, his wife sent him a message. It said, "Leave that innocent man alone. I've been very upset today because of a dream I had about him."

But the chief priests and leaders persuaded the crowd to ask for the release of Barabbas and the execution of Jesus.

The governor asked them, "Which of the two do you want me to free for you?"

They said, "Barabbas."

Pilate asked them, "Then what should I do with Jesus, who is called Christ?"

"He should be crucified!" they all said.

Pilate asked, "Why? What has he done wrong?"

But they began to shout loudly, "He should be crucified!"

Pilate saw that he was not getting anywhere. Instead, a riot was breaking out. So Pilate took some water and washed his hands in front of the crowd. He said, "I won't be guilty of killing this man. Do what you want!"

All the people answered, "The responsibility for killing him will rest on us and our children."

Then Pilate freed Barabbas for the people. But he had Jesus whipped and handed over to be crucified.

THE PEOPLE WANT JESUS CRUCIFIED
(JOHN 19:4–16A)

Pilate went outside again and told the Jews, "I'm bringing him out to you to let you know that I don't find this man guilty of anything." Jesus went outside. He was wearing the crown of thorns and the purple cape. Pilate said to the Jews, "Look, here's the man!"

When the chief priests and the guards saw Jesus, they shouted, "Crucify him! Crucify him!"

Pilate told them, "You take him and crucify him. I don't find this man guilty of anything."

The Jews answered Pilate, "We have a law, and by that law he must die because he claimed to be the Son of God."

When Pilate heard them say that, he became more afraid than ever. He went into the palace again and asked Jesus, "Where are you from?" But Jesus didn't answer him.

So Pilate said to Jesus, "Aren't you going to answer me? Don't you know that I have the authority to free you or to crucify you?"

Jesus answered Pilate, "You wouldn't have any authority over me if it hadn't been given to you from above. That's why the man who handed me over to you is guilty of a greater sin."

When Pilate heard what Jesus said, he wanted to free him. But the Jews shouted, "If you free this man, you're not a friend of the emperor. Anyone who claims to be a king is defying the emperor."

When Pilate heard what they said, he took Jesus outside and sat on the judge's seat in a place called Stone Pavement. (In Hebrew it is called *Gabbatha*.) The time was about six o'clock in the morning on the Friday of the Passover festival.

Pilate said to the Jews, "Look, here's your king!"

Then the Jews shouted, "Kill him! Kill him! Crucify him!"

Pilate asked them, "Should I crucify your king?"

The chief priests responded, "The emperor is the only king we have!"

Then Pilate handed Jesus over to them to be crucified.

So the soldiers took Jesus.

THE SOLDIERS MAKE FUN OF JESUS
(MATTHEW 27:27–31) ~see also Mark 15:16–19; John 19:1–3~

Then the governor's soldiers took Jesus into the palace and gathered the whole troop around him. They took off his clothes and put a bright red cape on him. They twisted some thorns into a crown, placed it on his head, and put a stick in his right hand. They knelt in front of him and made fun of him by saying, "Long live the king of the Jews!" After they had spit on him, they took the stick and kept hitting him on the head with it.

After the soldiers finished making fun of Jesus, they took off the cape and put his own clothes back on him. Then they led him away to crucify him.

JESUS IS CRUCIFIED

One of the few facts almost universally known about Jesus is that he died on a cross. Although periodically some debate arises as to whether or not he really died, the Gospel accounts are clear. Whipped, beaten, and speared in the side, Jesus was clearly dead to all observers at the scene. Soldiers trained in execution and familiar with the process were absolutely certain he was dead—their own lives were on the line if he was not. He was buried in a tomb secured with a Roman guard; the stage was set. Would this be the end? Was it all over?

THE CRUCIFIXION
(LUKE 23:26–28, JOHN 19:17–27, MARK
15:23–32) ~see also Matthew 27:31–44~

As the soldiers led Jesus away, they grabbed a man named Simon, who was from the city of Cyrene. Simon was coming into Jerusalem. They laid the cross on him and made him carry it behind Jesus.

A large crowd followed Jesus. The women in the crowd cried and sang funeral songs for him. Jesus turned to them and said, "You women of Jerusalem, don't cry for me! Rather, cry for yourselves and your children!"

He carried his own cross and went out of the city to a location called The Skull. (In Hebrew this place is called *Golgotha*.) The soldiers crucified Jesus and two other men there. Jesus was in the middle.

Pilate wrote a notice and put it on the cross. The notice read, "Jesus from Nazareth, the king of the Jews." Many Jews read this notice, because the place where Jesus was crucified was near the city. The notice was written in Hebrew, Latin, and Greek.

The chief priests of the Jewish people told Pilate, "Don't write, 'The king of the Jews!' Instead, write, 'He said that he is the king of the Jews.'"

Pilate replied, "I have written what I've written."

When the soldiers had crucified Jesus, they took his clothes and divided them four ways so that each soldier could have a share. His robe was left over. It didn't have a seam because it had been woven in one piece from top to bottom. The soldiers said to each other, "Let's not rip it apart. Let's throw dice to see who will get it." In this way the Scripture came true: "They divided my clothes among themselves. They threw dice for my clothing." So that's what the soldiers did.

Jesus' mother, her sister, Mary (the wife of Clopas), and Mary from Magdala were standing beside Jesus' cross. Jesus saw his mother and the disciple whom he loved standing there. He said to his mother, "Look, here's your son!" Then he said to the disciple, "Look, here's your mother!"

From that time on she lived with that disciple in his home.

They tried to give him wine mixed with a drug called myrrh, but he wouldn't take it. Next they crucified him. Then they divided his clothes among themselves by throwing dice to see what each one would get. It was nine in the morning when they crucified him. There was a written notice of the accusation against him. It read, "The king of the Jews."

They crucified two criminals with him, one on his right and the other on his left.

Those who passed by insulted him. They shook their heads and said, "What a joke! You were going to tear down God's temple and build it again in three days. Come down from the cross, and save yourself!" The chief priests and the scribes made fun of him among themselves in the same way. They said, "He saved others, but he can't save himself. Let the Messiah, the king of Israel, come down from the cross now so that we may see and believe." Even those who were crucified with him were insulting him.

The Crucifixion

Crucifixion was a common method of execution used by the Romans throughout the Empire. Intended not just to kill but also to thoroughly humiliate the prisoner, it was considered too brutal for Roman citizens and reserved for only the lowest type of criminal. As detailed in the Gospel accounts, the prisoner was brutally beaten, sometimes to the point of death, by a whip embedded with pieces of bone or metal. He was then forced to carry the cross-beam of the cross through the streets to a place outside the city where he would either be tied or nailed to the cross and raised up above the ground. While there was often a small piece of wood at the feet that served as a kind of support, the bulk of the body's weight was held up by the hands and arms, and death would often come slowly as the result of asphyxiation. Breaking the legs of the prisoners was a common way to hurry death, since prisoners could no longer support themselves and would be unable to move their diaphragm up and down in order to breathe. In the case of Jesus the soldiers did not break his legs but, having determined he was already dead, speared him in the side to make absolutely sure.

CRIMINALS TALK TO JESUS
(LUKE 23:39–43)

One of the criminals hanging there insulted Jesus by saying, "So you're really the Messiah, are you? Well, save yourself and us!"

But the other criminal scolded him: "Don't you fear God at all? Can't you see that you're condemned in the same way that he is? Our punishment is fair. We're getting what we deserve. But this man hasn't done anything wrong."

Then he said, "Jesus, remember me when you enter your kingdom."

Jesus said to him, "I can guarantee this truth: Today you will be with me in paradise."

JESUS DIES ON THE CROSS
(JOHN 19:28–29, MATTHEW 27:45–49, JOHN 19:30, MATTHEW 27:50–56, JOHN 19:31–37) ~see also Mark 15:33–41; Luke 23:44–49~

After this, when Jesus knew that everything had now been finished, he said, "I'm thirsty." He said this so that Scripture could finally be concluded.

A jar filled with vinegar was there. So the soldiers put a sponge soaked in the vinegar on a hyssop stick and held it to his mouth.

At noon darkness came over the whole land until three in the afternoon. About three o'clock Jesus cried out in a loud voice, "Eli, Eli, lema sabachthani?" which means, "My God, my God, why have you abandoned me?" When some of the people standing there heard him say that, they said, "He's calling Elijah." One of the men ran at once, took a sponge, and soaked it in some vinegar. Then he put it on a stick and offered Jesus a drink. The others said, "Leave him alone! Let's see if Elijah comes to save him."

After Jesus had taken the vinegar, he said, "It is finished!"

Then he bowed his head and died.

Then Jesus loudly cried out once again and gave up his life.

Suddenly, the curtain in the temple was split in two from top to bottom. The earth shook, and the rocks were split open. The tombs were opened, and the bodies of many holy people who had died came back to life. They came out of the tombs after he had come back to life, and they went into the holy city where they appeared to many people.

An army officer and those watching Jesus with him saw the earthquake and the other things happening. They were terrified and said, "Certainly, this was the Son of God!"

Many women were there watching from a distance. They had followed Jesus from Galilee and had always supported him. Among them were Mary from Magdala, Mary (the mother of James and Joseph), and the mother of Zebedee's sons.

Since it was Friday and the next day was an especially important day of worship, the Jews didn't want the bodies to stay on the crosses. So they asked Pilate to have the men's legs broken and their bodies removed. The soldiers broke the legs of the first man and then of the other man who had been crucified with Jesus.

When the soldiers came to Jesus and saw that he was already dead, they didn't break his legs. However, one of the soldiers stabbed Jesus' side with his spear, and blood and water immediately came out. The one who saw this is an eyewitness. What he says is true, and he knows that he is telling the truth so that you, too, will believe.

This happened so that the Scripture would come true: "None of his bones will be broken." Another Scripture passage says, "They will look at the person whom they have stabbed."

The Fulfillment of the Promise

Many prophecies come together in the death of Jesus. John's focus on the fact that none of his bones were broken is a reference to the perfection expected of the Passover lamb (Exod. 12:46) and recalls the prophecy regarding the Messiah found in Psalm 34:20. Clearly Jesus functioned as the ultimate Passover lamb. Mark's account draws attention to the temple and the destruction of the curtain. This supernatural act indicates that there is now no longer any separation between man and God, a point made explicitly in Hebrews 9. Luke sets the stage with a darkness that would have brought to mind imagery connected with the great and terrible day of the Lord prophesied in Joel and Amos. Luke also includes Jesus' quotation of Psalm 31:5, a psalm attributed to David and emphasizing complete submission to God's sovereign power. Matthew's narrative includes Jesus' cry of abandonment—a quotation taken from Psalm 22, which is filled with similarities to the circumstances surrounding Jesus' death. Taken together the scene fulfills the kind of scenario laid out in Isaiah 53 of the servant obediently enduring suffering in order to secure salvation for all.

JESUS IS BURIED AND THE CHIEF PRIESTS AND PHARISEES SECURE THE TOMB

(MATTHEW 27:57–66) ~see also Mark 15:42–47;
Luke 23:50–56; John 19:38–42~

In the evening a rich man named Joseph arrived. He was from the city of Arimathea and had become a disciple of Jesus. He went to Pilate and asked for the body of Jesus. Pilate ordered that it be given to him.

Joseph took the body and wrapped it in a clean linen cloth. Then he laid it in his own new tomb, which had been cut in a rock. After rolling a large stone against the door of the tomb, he went away. Mary from Magdala and the other Mary were sitting there, facing the tomb.

The next day, which was the day of worship, the chief priests and Pharisees gathered together and went to Pilate. They said, "Sir, we remember how that deceiver said while he was still alive, 'After three days I will be brought back to life.' Therefore, give the order to make the tomb secure until the third day. Otherwise, his disciples may steal him and say to the people, 'He has been brought back to life.' Then the last deception will be worse than the first."

Pilate told them, "You have the soldiers you want for guard duty. Go and make the tomb as secure as you know how."

So they went to secure the tomb. They placed a seal on the stone and posted the soldiers on guard duty.

JESUS IS RESURRECTED

Christianity rises and falls on the historical accuracy of the resurrection (1 Corinthians 15). If the resurrection did not happen, then our faith is pointless and we are to be pitied as fools. However, the evidence given in the Gospels is pretty compelling. Jesus appeared first to women, not something that the Gospel writers would have included if they were making the story up, since at the time women were considered unreliable witnesses (even the disciples didn't believe them). Jesus then appeared to some disciples on the road to Emmaus and then to the disciples hiding in a room. Thomas's doubts are recorded for us—doubt does not automatically lead to disbelief. Ultimately, after restoring Peter and giving much detailed instructions on what the disciples were to do next, Jesus ascended into heaven before their eyes, and the Church was launched into existence, blessed by Jesus and empowered by the Holy Spirit.

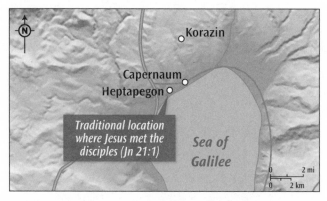

Resurrection Appearance in Galilee

JESUS COMES BACK TO LIFE
(JOHN 20:1–10) ~see also Matthew 28:1–10; Mark 16:1–8; Luke 24:1–12~

Early on Sunday morning, while it was still dark, Mary from Magdala went to the tomb. She saw that the stone had been removed from the tomb's entrance. So she ran to Simon Peter and the other disciple, whom Jesus loved. She told them, "They have removed the Lord from the tomb, and we don't know where they've put him."

So Peter and the other disciple headed for the tomb. The two were running side by side, but the other disciple ran faster than Peter and came to the tomb first. He bent over and looked inside the tomb. He saw the strips of linen lying there but didn't go inside.

Simon Peter arrived after him and went into the tomb. He saw the strips of linen lying there. He also saw the cloth that had been on Jesus' head. It wasn't lying with the strips of linen but was rolled up separately. Then the other disciple, who arrived at the tomb first, went inside. He saw and believed. They didn't know yet what Scripture meant when it said that Jesus had to come back to life. So the disciples went back home.

The Importance of the Resurrection

Paul is clear that without the resurrection there is no Christianity (1 Corinthians 15). Although the Bible records a few instances of individuals being raised from the dead, there are no records of anyone ever being resurrected in the manner in which Jesus was raised. While Lazarus and others were brought back to life for a short time, their deaths were still inevitable. The character of the resurrection was different. As Paul says in Colossians, we died with Christ for our sins and were raised with Christ into new life (Col. 2:12–15). Without the resurrection there is no power over death, there is no victory over Satan. It was the resurrection that proved everything Jesus had claimed throughout his ministry. It was the resurrection that secured his divinity and changed the world forever. It was the resurrection that announced the dawning of the kingdom of God and turned the tide against the dreadful power of sin introduced by Adam and Eve.

JESUS APPEARS TO MARY FROM MAGDALA
(JOHN 20:11–18)

Mary, however, stood there and cried as she looked at the tomb. As she cried, she bent over and looked inside. She saw two angels in white clothes. They were sitting where the body of Jesus had been lying. One angel was where Jesus' head had been, and the other was where his feet had been. The angels asked her why she was crying.

Mary told them, "They have removed my Lord, and I don't know where they've put him."

After she said this, she turned around and saw Jesus standing there. However, she didn't know that it was Jesus. Jesus asked her, "Why are you crying? Who are you looking for?"

Mary thought it was the gardener speaking to her. So she said to him, "Sir, if you carried him away, tell me where you have put him, and I'll remove him."

Jesus said to her, "Mary!"

Mary turned around and said to him in Hebrew, "Rabboni!" (This word means "teacher.")

Jesus told her, "Don't hold on to me. I have not yet gone to the Father. But go to my brothers and sisters and tell them, 'I am going to my Father and your Father, to my God and your God.'"

Mary from Magdala went to the disciples and told them, "I have seen the Lord." She also told them what he had said to her.

JESUS APPEARS TO THE WOMEN
(MATTHEW 28:8–10)

They hurried away from the tomb with fear and great joy and ran to tell his disciples.

Suddenly, Jesus met them and greeted them. They went up to him, bowed down to worship him, and took hold of his feet.

Then Jesus said to them, "Don't be afraid! Go, tell my followers to go to Galilee. There they will see me."

THE GUARDS REPORT TO THE CHIEF PRIESTS
(MATTHEW 28:11–15)

While the women were on their way, some of the guards went into the city. They told the chief priests everything that had happened.

The chief priests gathered together with the leaders and agreed on a plan. They gave the soldiers a large amount of money and told them to say that Jesus' disciples had come at night and had stolen his body while they were sleeping. They added, "If the governor hears about it, we'll take care of it, and you'll have nothing to worry about."

The soldiers took the money and did as they were told. Their story has been spread among the Jewish people to this day.

JESUS APPEARS TO DISCIPLES ON A ROAD TO EMMAUS
(LUKE 24:13–35)

On the same day, two of Jesus' disciples were going to a village called Emmaus. It was about seven miles from Jerusalem. They were talking to each other about everything that had happened.

While they were talking, Jesus approached them and began walking with them. Although they saw him, they didn't recognize him.

He asked them, "What are you discussing?"

They stopped and looked very sad. One of them, Cleopas, replied, "Are you the only one in Jerusalem who doesn't know what has happened recently?"

"What happened?" he asked.

They said to him, "We were discussing what happened to Jesus from Nazareth. He was a powerful prophet in what he did and said in the sight of God and all the people. Our chief priests and rulers had him condemned to death and crucified. We were hoping that he was the one who would free Israel. What's more, this is now the third day since everything happened. Some of the women from our group startled us. They went to the tomb early this morning and didn't find his body. They told us that they had seen angels who said that he's alive. Some of our men went to the tomb and found it empty, as the women had said, but they didn't see him."

Then Jesus said to them, "How foolish you are! You're so slow to believe everything the prophets said! Didn't the Messiah have to suffer these things and enter into his glory?" Then he began with Moses' Teachings and the Prophets to explain to them what was said about him throughout the Scriptures.

When they came near the village where they were going, Jesus acted as if he were going farther. They urged him, "Stay with us! It's getting late, and the day is almost over." So he went to stay with them.

While he was at the table with them, he took bread and blessed it. He broke the bread and gave it to them. Then their eyes were opened, and they recognized him. But he vanished from their sight.

They said to each other, "Weren't we excited when he talked with us on the road and opened up the meaning of the Scriptures for us?"

That same hour they went back to Jerusalem. They found the eleven apostles and those who were with them gathered together. They were saying, "The Lord has really come back to life and has appeared to Simon."

Then the two disciples told what had happened on the road and how they had recognized Jesus when he broke the bread.

JESUS APPEARS TO THE DISCIPLES
(JOHN 20:19–23)

That Sunday evening, the disciples were together behind locked doors because they were afraid of the Jews. Jesus stood among them and said to them, "Peace be with you!" When he said this, he showed them his hands and his side. The disciples were glad to see the Lord.

Jesus said to them again, "Peace be with you! As the Father has sent me, so I am sending you." After he had said this, he breathed on the disciples and said, "Receive the Holy Spirit. Whenever you forgive sins, they are forgiven. Whenever you don't forgive them, they are not forgiven."

JESUS APPEARS TO THOMAS
(JOHN 20:24–31)

Thomas, one of the twelve apostles, who was called Didymus, wasn't with them when Jesus came. The other disciples told him, "We've seen the Lord."

Thomas told them, "I refuse to believe this unless I see the nail marks in his hands, put my fingers into them, and put my hand into his side."

A week later Jesus' disciples were again in the house, and Thomas was with them. Even though the doors were locked, Jesus stood among them and said, "Peace be with you!" Then Jesus said to Thomas, "Put your finger here, and look at my hands. Take your hand, and put it into my side. Stop doubting, and believe."

Thomas responded to Jesus, "My Lord and my God!"

Jesus said to Thomas, "You believe because you've seen me. Blessed are those who haven't seen me but believe."

Jesus performed many other miracles that his disciples saw. Those miracles are not written in this book. But these miracles have been written so that you will believe that Jesus is the Messiah, the Son of God, and so that you will have life by believing in him.

Dealing with Our Doubts

Contrary to those who claim Christianity requires blind assent, Jesus himself is quite understanding and tolerant of the doubts and concerns of his disciples. It is telling that even those who had walked with him over so many miles and for so many years did not recognize him as they walked down the road to Emmaus. Were the Gospel writers trying to create a legend from scratch they would have been quick to point out both the eager expectations of the disciples for his resurrection (instead they all fled) and the immediate acceptance of what had happened (instead many of them had doubts and were confused). The only reason to include these details is if they were true. Thomas was not being irreverent—he simply wanted more proof. This, Jesus was glad to give. Although Jesus had sternly rebuked the Pharisees when they asked for a sign, in the case of those who already believe and trust in him Jesus appears to be both understanding and willing to help. Our attitude should be like the father of a demon-possessed boy who said to Jesus, "I believe! Help my lack of faith" (Mark 9:24).

JESUS APPEARS TO HIS DISCIPLES AGAIN
(JOHN 21:1–14)

Later, by the Sea of Tiberias, Jesus showed himself again to the disciples. This is what happened. Simon Peter, Thomas (called Didymus), Nathanael from Cana in Galilee, Zebedee's sons, and two other disciples of Jesus were together. Simon Peter said to the others, "I'm going fishing."

They told him, "We're going with you."

They went out in a boat but didn't catch a thing that night. As the sun was rising, Jesus stood on the shore. The disciples didn't realize that it was Jesus.

Jesus asked them, "Friends, haven't you caught any fish?"

They answered him, "No, we haven't."

He told them, "Throw the net out on the right side of the boat, and you'll catch some." So they threw the net out and were unable to pull it in because so many fish were in it.

The disciple whom Jesus loved said to Peter, "It's the Lord." When Simon Peter heard that it was the Lord, he put back on the clothes that he had taken off and jumped into the sea. The other disciples came with the boat and dragged the net full of fish. They weren't far from the shore, only about 100 yards.

When they went ashore, they saw a fire with a fish lying on the coals, and they saw a loaf of bread.

Jesus told them, "Bring some of the fish you've just caught." Simon Peter got into the boat and pulled the net ashore. Though the net was filled with 153 large fish, it was not torn.

Jesus told them, "Come, have breakfast." None of the disciples dared to ask him who he was. They knew he was the Lord. Jesus took the bread, gave it to them, and did the same with the fish.

This was the third time that Jesus showed himself to the disciples after he had come back to life.

JESUS SPEAKS WITH PETER
(JOHN 21:15–25)

After they had eaten breakfast, Jesus asked Simon Peter, "Simon, son of John, do you love me more than the other disciples do?"

Peter answered him, "Yes, Lord, you know that I love you."

Jesus told him, "Feed my lambs."

Jesus asked him again, a second time, "Simon, son of John, do you love me?"

Peter answered him, "Yes, Lord, you know that I love you."

Jesus told him, "Take care of my sheep."

Jesus asked him a third time, "Simon, son of John, do you love me?"

Peter felt sad because Jesus had asked him a third time, "Do you love me?" So Peter said to him, "Lord, you know everything. You know that I love you."

Jesus told him, "Feed my sheep. I can guarantee this truth: When you were young, you would get ready to go where you wanted. But when you're old, you will stretch out your hands, and someone else will get you ready to take you where you don't want to go." Jesus said this to show by what kind of death Peter would bring glory to God. After saying this, Jesus told Peter, "Follow me!"

Peter turned around and saw the disciple whom Jesus loved. That disciple was following them. He was the one who leaned against Jesus' chest at the supper and asked, "Lord, who is going to betray you?" When Peter saw him, he asked Jesus, "Lord, what about him?"

Jesus said to Peter, "If I want him to live until I come again, how does that concern you? Follow me!" So a rumor that that disciple wouldn't die spread among Jesus' followers. But Jesus didn't say that he wouldn't die. What Jesus said was, "If I want him to live until I come again, how does that concern you?"

This disciple was an eyewitness of these things and wrote them down. We know that what he says is true.

Jesus also did many other things. If every one of them were written down,

I suppose the world wouldn't have enough room for the books that would be written.

JESUS GIVES INSTRUCTIONS TO THE DISCIPLES
(MATTHEW 28:16–20)

The eleven disciples went to the mountain in Galilee where Jesus had told them to go. When they saw him, they bowed down in worship, though some had doubts.

When Jesus came near, he spoke to them. He said, "All authority in heaven and on earth has been given to me. So wherever you go, make disciples of all nations: Baptize them in the name of the Father, and of the Son, and of the Holy Spirit. Teach them to do everything I have commanded you.

"And remember that I am always with you until the end of time."

JESUS APPEARS TO THE DISCIPLES IN JERUSALEM
(LUKE 24:44–49)

Then he said to them, "These are the words I spoke to you while I was still with you. I told you that everything written about me in Moses' Teachings, the Prophets, and the Psalms had to come true." Then he opened their minds to understand the Scriptures. He said to them, "Scripture says that the Messiah would suffer and that he would come back to life on the third day. Scripture also says that by the authority of Jesus people would be told to turn to God and change the way they think and act so that their sins will be forgiven. This would be told to people from all nations, beginning in the city of Jerusalem. You are witnesses to these things.

"I'm sending you what my Father promised. Wait here in the city until you receive power from heaven."

JESUS ASCENDS INTO HEAVEN
(LUKE 24:50–53)

Then Jesus took them to a place near Bethany. There he raised his hands and blessed them. While he was blessing them, he left them and was taken to heaven.

The disciples worshiped him and were overjoyed as they went back to Jerusalem. They were always in the temple, where they praised God.

Where Is Jesus Now?

The Bible is clear that Jesus now sits at the right hand of God, a position of authority and honor (Rom. 8:34; 1 Tim. 2:5; 1 John 2:1). His work is to intercede on behalf of his people and to guide and care for them. As the author of Hebrews says, he is our "chief priest," enabling us to "go confidently to the throne of God's kindness to receive mercy and find kindness, which will help us at the right time" (Heb. 4:16). There is no longer any need for an earthly temple with priests and sacrifices, since Jesus was the ultimate sacrifice and through his death and resurrection did away with the entire sacrificial system. From heaven Jesus is still very active in the growth and development of his people and his church and works through the Holy Spirit to lead us into lives of holiness and purity. However, the Bible is also clear that Jesus' work is not yet done, for one day he will return in order to judge the world and bring the kingdom of God into total completion.

BIOGRAPHIES OF THE GOSPEL WRITERS

MATTHEW

Matthew, the son of Alphaeus, was a tax collector before Jesus called him to be a disciple (Matt. 9:9–13). Also known as Levi, Matthew served under King Herod (Antipas) and collected taxes in Galilee, probably on the road from Damascus to the Mediterranean. But when Jesus asked him to follow, Matthew gave up everything to become a disciple.

Matthew probably wrote his Gospel thirty years after Jesus' death (around AD 60). He wrote it with a Jewish audience in mind. He hoped to authenticate Jesus' claim as Messiah by cataloguing Jesus' genealogy, sermons, and miracles.

JOHN MARK

John Mark was the cousin of Barnabas, the missionary who traveled with Paul, and also a companion of the apostle Peter. Although he bore a Roman name, John Mark came from a Jewish family and was a native of Jerusalem. The home of Mark's mother was a meeting place for believers (Acts 12:12). Mark is believed to be the young man who fled from the garden of Gethsemane when Jesus was arrested (Mark 14:51–52).

After traveling on a missionary journey with Paul and Barnabas and leaving them early in the trip, Mark was the cause of a disagreement between Paul and Barnabas (Acts 15:36–40). Paul didn't want to take Mark on another journey, but Barnabas did. Apparently, Mark was later forgiven by Paul (Col. 4:10–11; 2 Tim. 4:11).

Mark's Gospel is believed to be the first Gospel, having been written between AD 50 and 60.

LUKE

Luke was the only Gentile Gospel writer. He also wrote the book of Acts, the great record of the beginning of the Christian church. Luke, a physician from Antioch, traveled with Paul, starting in his second missionary journey. Luke was also a historian, one who carefully recorded the early events of Jesus' life and their unique position in history.

Luke is the one credited by Paul for remaining with Paul when all others deserted him during his imprisonment (2 Tim. 4:11). That Paul referred to him as "my dear friend Luke, the physician," not only indicates his esteem for Luke, but also suggests that Luke gave medical care to Paul (Col. 4:14). He later is referred to as a fellow-worker in Philemon, indicating that Luke's contribution to Paul's gospel work was not merely related to the medical.

Luke probably wrote his Gospel after Paul's death in AD 64. He also had a Gentile audience in mind. According to tradition, Luke died in Achaia at the age of 84.

JOHN

John, the son of Zebedee, was one of the first of the twelve disciples chosen by Jesus (Matt. 4:21–22). He was a fisherman by trade and left that profession along with his brother, James.

Throughout the Gospel that bears his name, John is known as the disciple whom Jesus loved (John 13:23; 19:26). John and his brother James also were known by Jesus as "Thunderbolts" (Mark 3:17), most likely because the two were high-spirited Galileans, whose zeal was sometimes misdirected and undisciplined (Luke 9:49, 51–55). John is one of the three disciples most often mentioned with Jesus. He was one of the three who saw Jesus transfigured (Matthew 17) and the raising of Jairus's daughter from the dead (Mark 5). John also was one of the three disciples Jesus took with him to the garden of Gethsemane before his arrest. John also ran with Peter to the tomb on that first Easter morning and was present when the risen Jesus presented himself to seven disciples by the sea of Tiberias.

John wrote the Gospel that bears his name, along with the three epistles and the book of Revelation. The latter was written during John's exile on the island of Patmos.

TIMELINE OF JESUS' LIFE & MINISTRY

JESUS' CHILDHOOD

Date	Event	Place	Scripture
6/5 BC	Birth of Jesus	Bethlehem	Matt. 1:18–25; Luke 2:1–7
	Visit by shepherds	Bethlehem	Luke 2:8–20
	Presentation in the temple	Jerusalem	Luke 2:21–40
	The wise men visit	Bethlehem	Matt. 2:1–12
	Escape to Egypt	Nile Delta	Matt. 2:13–18
	Return to Nazareth	Lower Galilee	Matt. 2:19–23
AD 7/8	Jesus visits the temple	Jerusalem	Luke 2:41–52

JESUS' MINISTRY BEGINS

Date	Event	Place	Scripture
AD 26	Jesus is baptized	Jordan River	Matt. 3:13–17; Mark 1:9–11; Luke 3:21–23; John 1:29–34
	The temptation of Jesus	Desert	Matt. 4:1–11; Mark 1:12–13; Luke 4:1–13
	Jesus' first miracle	Cana	John 2:1–11
AD 27	Jesus clears the temple	Jerusalem	John 2:13–22

Date	Event	Place	Scripture
AD 27	Jesus talks with Nicodemus	Jerusalem	John 3:1–21
	Jesus talks with a Samaritan woman	Samaria	John 4:1–42
	Jesus heals an official's son	Cana	John 4:46–54
	Nazareth rejects Jesus	Nazareth	Luke 4:16–30

JESUS' MINISTRY GROWS

Date	Event	Place	Scripture
	Four fishermen become Jesus' followers	Sea of Galilee at Capernaum	Matt. 4:18–22; Mark 1:16–20; Luke 5:1–11
	Jesus heals Peter's mother-in-law and others	Capernaum	Matt. 8:14–17; Mark 1:29–34; Luke 4:38–41
	Jesus begins his first preaching trip	The region of Galilee	Matt. 4:23–25; Mark 1:35–39; Luke 4:42–44
	Matthew follows Jesus	Capernaum	Matt. 9:9–13; Mark 2:13–17; Luke 5:27–32
AD 28	Jesus chooses the twelve disciples	Capernaum	Matt. 10:1–4; Mark 3:13–19; Luke 6:12–16
	Jesus preaches the "Sermon on the Mountain"	Capernaum	Matt. 5:1–7:29; Luke 6:20–49
	A sinful woman receives forgiveness	Capernaum	Luke 7:36–50
	Jesus travels again through Galilee	The region of Galilee	Luke 8:1–3
	Jesus tells parables about the kingdom of God	Sea of Galilee	Matt. 13:1–52; Mark 4:1–34; Luke 8:4–18

Date	Event	Place	Scripture
AD 28	Jesus calms the storm	Sea of Galilee	Matt. 8:23–27; Mark 4:35–41; Luke 8:22–25
	Jesus brings Jairus's daughter back to life	Capernaum	Matt. 9:18–26; Mark 5:21–43; Luke 8:40–56
	Jesus sends out the twelve to preach and heal	The region of Galilee	Matt. 9:35–11:1; Mark 6:7–13; Luke 9:1–6

JESUS FACES GROWING OPPOSITION

	Herod kills John the Baptist	Machaerus	Matt. 14:1–12; Mark 6:14–29; Luke 9:7–9
AD 29	Jesus feeds 5,000	Near Bethsaida	Matt. 14:13–21; Mark 6:30–44; Luke 9:10–17; John 6:1–14
	Jesus walks on the water	Near Bethsaida	Matt. 14:22–33; Mark 6:45–52; John 6:16–21
	Jesus withdraws to Tyre and Sidon	Tyre and Sidon	Matt. 15:21–28; Mark 7:24–30
	Jesus feeds 4,000	Near the Sea of Galilee	Matt. 15:32–39; Mark 8:1–10
	Peter declares his belief about Jesus	Caesarea Philippi	Matt. 16:13–20; Mark 8:27–30; Luke 9:18–21
	Jesus predicts his death	Caesarea Philippi	Matt. 16:21–23; Mark 8:31–33; Luke 9:22
	Moses and Elijah appear with Jesus	Caesarea Philippi	Matt. 17:1–13; Mark 9:2–13; Luke 9:28–36
	Jesus pays his temple taxes	Capernaum	Matt. 17:24–27
	Jesus attends the Festival of Booths	Jerusalem	John 7:11–53
	Jesus gives sight to a blind man	Jerusalem	John 9:1–41

Date	Event	Place	Scripture
AD 29	Jesus visits Mary and Martha	Bethany	Luke 10:38–42
	Jesus brings Lazarus back to life	Bethany	John 11:1–44
AD 30	Jesus begins his last trip to Jerusalem	The border between Galilee and Samaria	Luke 17:11
	Jesus blesses the children	Across the Jordan	Matt. 19:13–15; Mark 10:13–16; Luke 18:15–17
	Jesus talks about eternal life to an official	Across the Jordan	Matt. 19:16–30; Mark 10:17–31; Luke 18:18–30
	Jesus again predicts his death and resurrection	Near the Jordan	Matt. 20:17–19; Mark 10:32–34; Luke 18:31–34
	Jesus gives sight to Bartimaeus	Jericho	Matt. 20:29–34; Mark 10:46–52; Luke 18:35–43
	Jesus meets Zacchaeus	Jericho	Luke 19:1–10
	The Jewish council plans to kill Jesus	Jerusalem	John 11:45–57

JESUS' LAST WEEK

Date	Event	Place	Scripture
Sunday	The King comes to Jerusalem	Bethphage, Bethany at the Mount of Olives, Jerusalem	Matt. 21:1–11; Mark 11:1–10; Luke 19:28–44; John 12:12–19
Monday	Jesus curses the fig tree	Jerusalem	Matt. 21:18–19; Mark 11:12–14
	Jesus throws out the moneychangers	Jerusalem	Matt. 21:12–17; Mark 11:15–19; Luke 19:45–48

Date	Event	Place	Scripture
Tuesday	Jesus' authority is challenged	Jerusalem	Matt. 21:23–27; Mark 11:27–33; Luke 20:1–8
	Jesus teaches in the temple	Jerusalem	Matt. 21:28–23:39; Mark 12:1–44; Luke 20:9–21:4
	A woman prepares Jesus' body for the tomb	Bethany	Matt. 26:6–13; Mark 14:3–9; John 12:2–8
Wednesday	Judas plans to betray Jesus	Jerusalem	Matt. 26:14–16; Mark 14:10–11; Luke 22:3–6
Thursday	The Lord's Supper	Jerusalem	Matt. 26:17–29; Mark 14:12–25; Luke 22:7–20; John 13:1–38
	Jesus comforts his disciples	Jerusalem	John 14:1–16:33
	Jesus in Gethsemane	Jerusalem	Matt. 26:36–46; Mark 14:32–42; Luke 22:39–46
Thursday night and Friday	Jesus is arrested and faces trial	Jerusalem	Matt. 26:47–27:26; Mark 14:43–15:15; Luke 22:47–23:25; John 18:1–19:16
Friday	Jesus is crucified and dies	Golgotha	Matt. 27:27–56; Mark 15:16–41; Luke 23:26–49; John 19:16–30
	Jesus is buried	Joseph's tomb	Matt. 27:57–66; Mark 15:42–47; Luke 23:50–56; John 19:31–42

AFTER JESUS' RESURRECTION

Date	Event	Place	Scripture
Sunday	Jesus comes back to life	Jerusalem	Matt. 28:1–10; Mark 16:1–8; Luke 24:1–12; John 20:1–10
	Jesus appears to Mary from Magdala and others	Jerusalem	Mark 16:9–11; John 20:11–18

Date	Event	Place	Scripture
Sunday	Jesus appears to disciples on a road to Emmaus	Outside Jerusalem	Mark 16:12–13; Luke 24:13–35
	Jesus appears to eleven apostles	Jerusalem	Mark 16:14; Luke 24:36–43; John 20:19–23
One week later	Jesus appears to Thomas	Jerusalem	John 20:24–29
	Jesus appears to his disciples again	Sea of Galilee	John 21:1–25
40 days later	Jesus ascends to his Father in heaven	Mount of Olives	Matt. 28:16–20; Mark 16:15–20; Luke 24:44–53

JESUS' PROMISES

Promise	Bible Reference
The presence and guidance of the Holy Spirit, who will teach us about Jesus.	Luke 12:11–12
	John 14:16–17
	John 14:26
"At that time the Holy Spirit will teach you what you must say."—Luke 12:12	John 15:26
	John 16:7–11
	John 16:13–14
	John 20:21–22
Ask and it will be given to you.	Matthew 7:7–8
	Matthew 18:19–20
"Everyone who asks will receive. The one who searches will find, and for the one who knocks, the door will be opened."	Matthew 21:22
	Luke 11:9–10
	John 14:12–14
—Matthew 7:8	John 15:7
	John 16:24
God is our Protector; he is with us always.	Matthew 28:18–20
	John 14:18
"And remember that I am always with you until the end of time."—Matthew 28:20b	John 17:15
Jesus will give joy, peace, and rest to those who come to him and follow his commands.	Matthew 5:9
	Matthew 11:28–30
	John 14:1–3
"I've told you this so that my peace will be with you. In the world you'll have trouble. But cheer up! I have overcome the world."—John 16:33	John 14:27
	John 15:9–11
	John 16:33

God is our Provider; seek God's kingdom and he will provide for you.	Matthew 6:31–33 Luke 11:13 Luke 12:22–32
"Don't be afraid, little flock. Your Father is pleased to give you the kingdom."—Luke 12:32	John 1:16 John 6:35 John 10:10
Those who believe in Jesus will have eternal life and live with him.	Luke 10:25–28 Luke 18:18–30 John 3:16
"God loved the world this way: He gave his only Son so that everyone who believes in him will not die but will have eternal life."—John 3:16	John 4:13–14 John 5:24 John 6:40 John 10:27–29 John 11:25–26
With God, all things are possible.	Matthew 19:16–30 Mark 10:17–31
"It's impossible for people to save themselves, but it's not impossible for God to save them. Everything is possible for God."—Mark 10:27	Luke 18:18–30
God loves us.	John 3:16 John 14:15, 21, 23–24
"The Father loves you because you have loved me and have believed that I came from God."—John 16:27	John 16:27
The sacrifice of Jesus is for everyone, not just "the righteous."	Matthew 9:12–13 Matthew 20:28
"It's the same way with the Son of Man. He didn't come so that others could serve him. He came to serve and to give his life as a ransom for many people."—Mark 10:45	Mark 10:45

JESUS' PARABLES

Parable Description	Biblical References
Light under a Basket	Matthew 5:14–16 Mark 4:21–25 Luke 8:16–18 Luke 11:33–36
Build on the Rock	Matthew 7:24–27
New Cloth	Matthew 9:16 Mark 2:21 Luke 5:36
New Wine, Old Wineskins	Matthew 9:17 Mark 2:22 Luke 5:37–39
Mustard Seed	Matthew 13:31–32 Mark 4:30–32 Luke 13:18–19
Pearl of Great Price	Matthew 13:45–46
Story about a Farmer	Matthew 13:1–13 Mark 4:1–20 Luke 8:4–15

Parable Description	Biblical References
Weeds in the Wheat	Matthew 13:24–30 Matthew 13:36–43
Yeast (The Leaven)	Matthew 13:33 Luke 13:20–21
The Treasure	Matthew 13:44
The Fishing Net	Matthew 13:47–50
Seeds That Grow	Mark 4:26–29
Lost Sheep	Matthew 18:12–14 Luke 15:3–7
Unmerciful Servant (The Unforgiving Servant)	Matthew 18:21–35
Workers in the Vineyard (in the Harvest)	Matthew 20:1–16
Two Sons	Matthew 21:28–32
Vineyard and the Tenants (The Evil Farmers)	Matthew 21:33–46 Mark 12:1–12 Luke 20:9–19
Wedding Banquet (The Wedding Feast)	Matthew 22:1–14
Fig Tree	Matthew 24:32–35 Mark 13:28–31 Luke 21:29–33
The Wise and Faithful Servants	Matthew 24:45–51 Luke 12:42–48
The Ten Bridesmaids	Matthew 25:1–13

Parable Description	Biblical References
Three Servants	Matthew 25:14–30
Household Watching (The Traveling Owner of the House)	Mark 13:32–37
Debtors (The Forgiven Debts)	Luke 7:41–43
Good Samaritan	Luke 10:25–37
The Friend at Midnight	Luke 11:5–8
Rich Fool	Luke 12:16–21
Watchful Servants (Faithful Servant)	Luke 12:35–40
Faithful Steward	Luke 12:42–48
The Fruitless Tree	Luke 13:6–9
The Wedding Feast (The Guests)	Luke 14:7–11
Great Banquet (Great Festival)	Luke 14:15–24
Cost of Being a Disciple (Tower Builder [28–30] and King at War [31–32])	Luke 14:25–33
Lost Coin	Luke 15:8–10
The Lost Son (The Prodigal Son)	Luke 15:11–32
Shrewd Manager (The Unjust Steward)	Luke 16:1–13
Rich Man and Lazarus	Luke 16:19–31
Master and Servant (The Servant's Role)	Luke 17:7–10

Parable Description	Biblical References
Widow (The Unjust Judge)	Luke 18:1–8
Pharisee and the Tax Collector	Luke 18:9–14
Ten Minas (The Nobleman's Servants)	Luke 19:11–27

JESUS' RADICAL IDEAS AND TEACHINGS

Teaching	Bible Reference
Settle disagreements and legal matters privately	Matthew 5:25–26 Luke 12:57–59
Turn the other cheek (do not seek revenge or live by "an eye for an eye")	Matthew 5:38–42 Luke 6:29–31
Love and forgive your enemies	Matthew 5:43–48 Luke 6:27–28, 32–36
Let your prayers, fasting, and good deeds go unnoticed; do not seek attention for them	Matthew 6:1–8, 16–18
Do not pursue earthly wealth, honor or possessions, store up treasures in heaven; things of this world will not last	Matthew 6:19–24 Matthew 19:16–26 Matthew 19:30 Matthew 20:1–16 Mark 9:43–49 Mark 10:17–27 Mark 12:41–44 Luke 6:20–26 Luke 12:13–21 Luke 12:33–34 Luke 16:10–13 Luke 18:18–27 Luke 21:1–4

Teaching	Bible Reference
Trust God for provision; do not worry or be consumed by doubt, pursuit of wealth	Matthew 6:25–34 Luke 12:22–31
Do not make judgments about others; the same standards will be applied to you	Matthew 7:1–5 Luke 6:37–42 John 8:1–11
Jesus ate and spent time with tax collectors and sinners	Matthew 9:10–13 Luke 5:27–32 Luke 7:26–50 Luke 15:1–2 Luke 19:1–9
Do not worry about being persecuted; the Lord will sustain you	Matthew 10:16–23 Luke 21:12–19
Family in Christ is more important than biological family	Matthew 10:34–39 Matthew 12:46–50 Matthew 19:28–30 Mark 3:31–35 Mark 10:29–31 Luke 8:19–21 Luke 9:59–62 Luke 14:25–27 Luke 18:28–30 John 3:5–6
Following Christ supersedes laws and tradition, even religious laws and traditions	Matthew 12:1–14 Matthew 15:1–11 Matthew 19:1–9 Matthew 23:23–24 Mark 2:23–28 Mark 7:14–23 Luke 6:1–5 Luke 13:10–17 Luke 14:1–6 John 5:5–15 John 7:21–24 John 9:13–16

Teaching	Bible Reference
Religious leaders can be false teachers, hypocrites	Matthew 16:5–12
	Matthew 21:33–46
	Matthew 23:1–8
	Matthew 23:27–32
	Mark 7:5–13
	Luke 11:37–54
	Luke 12:1–3
	Luke 18:9–14
	Luke 20:45–47
Jesus rebuked his disciples when they tried to protect him from suffering	Matthew 16:21–23
	Mark 8:31–33
People must become humble, like children, to enter the kingdom of heaven	Matthew 18:1–4
	Matthew 19:13–15
	Mark 9:36–37
	Mark 10:13–16
	Luke 9:46–48
	Luke 18:15–17
Matters of sin should be dealt with within the church; people are accountable to their fellow Christ-followers	Matthew 18:15–17
Forgive those who sin against you, just as you have been forgiven a far greater debt	Matthew 18:21–35
The first shall be last, and the last shall be first; put aside selfish pursuits and put the needs of others first	Matthew 16:24–26
	Matthew 19:30
	Matthew 20:1–16
	Matthew 20:20–28
	Matthew 21:28–32
	Matthew 23:11
	Mark 8:34–38
	Mark 9:33–35
	Mark 10:44–45
	Luke 9:23–25
	Luke 10:25–37
	Luke 13:29–30
	Luke 14:7–11
	Luke 22:24–30
	John 13:1–17

Teaching	Bible Reference
Loving God and loving others are the greatest commandments	Matthew 22:34–40 Mark 12:28–34
Great things can be accomplished by a small amount of faith	Mark 9:14–29 Mark 11:20–25 Luke 7:1–10 Luke 17:5–6
Do good to the poor, crippled, lame and blind	Luke 14:12–14

ENCOUNTERS WITH JESUS

Description (Who?)	Bible Reference
The Wise Men	Matthew 2:1–12
John the Baptist	Matthew 3:13–17 Matthew 11:1–19 Mark 1:9–11 Luke 3:21–22 John 1:29–34
Satan (temptation of Jesus)	Matthew 4:1–11 Mark 1:12–13 Luke 4:1–13
The first disciples	Matthew 4:18–22 Mark 1:16–20 Luke 5:1–11 John 1:35–50
A man with a skin disease	Matthew 8:1–4 Mark 1:40–45 Luke 5:12–14
A believing army officer	Matthew 8:5–13 Luke 7:1–10 John 4:43–54

Description (Who?)	Bible Reference
Peter's mother-in-law	Matthew 8:14–15
	Mark 1:29–31
	Luke 4:38–39
Demon-possessed people	Matthew 8:28–34
	Matthew 17:14–20
	Mark 1:21–28
	Mark 5:1–20
	Mark 9:14–27
	Luke 4:31–36
	Luke 8:26–39
	Luke 9:37–43
A paralyzed man	Matthew 9:1–8
	Mark 2:1–12
	Luke 5:17–26
Matthew, the tax collector	Matthew 9:9–13
A woman with chronic bleeding	Matthew 9:20–22
	Mark 5:24–34
	Luke 8:43–48
Jairus, a synagogue leader	Matthew 9:18, 19, 23–26
	Mark 5:21–24, 35–43
	Luke 8:40–42a, 49–56
Two blind men	Matthew 9:27–31

Description (Who?)	Bible Reference
Twelve Disciples	
Instructions for ministry	Matthew 10 (entire chapter)
Ask about the greatest in the kingdom	Matthew 18:1–5
	Mark 9:33–37
	Luke 9:46–48
Jesus predicts his death	Matthew 20:17–19
	Mark 10:32–34
	Luke 18:31–34
	John 12:20–36
Jesus tells signs of the end of the age	Matthew 24 (entire chapter)
	Mark 13 (entire chapter)
	Luke 21:5–38
The Lord's Supper	Matthew 26:17–30
	Mark 14:12–26
	Luke 22:7–38
With Jesus in Gethsemane	Matthew 26:36–46
	Mark 14:32–42
	Luke 22:39–46
Jesus gives the Great Commission	Matthew 28:16–20
Appointing of the twelve disciples	Mark 3:13–19
	Luke 6:12–16
Jesus calms the storm	Matthew 8:23–27
	Mark 4:35–41
	Luke 8:22–25
Jesus walks on water	Matthew 14:22–33
	Mark 6:45–51
	John 6:16–21
Jesus teaches them how to pray	Matthew 7:7–11
	Luke 11:1–13
Appears to them after resurrection, ascension	Luke 24:36–53
	John 20:19–23
Jesus washed his disciples' feet	John 13:1–17
Post-resurrection miraculous catch of fish	John 21:1–14
Man with a shriveled hand	Matthew 12:9–14
	Mark 3:1–6
	Luke 6:6–11

Description (Who?)	Bible Reference
Jewish Religious Leaders (The Pharisees, Sadducees, the Sanhedrin, chief priests, and elders of the people)	Matthew 12:22–37
	Matthew 12:38–45
	Matthew 15:1–14
	Matthew 16:1–4
	Matthew 19:3–12
	Matthew 21:23–46
	Matthew 22:15–46
	Matthew 26:57–68
	Mark 2:15–17, 23–28
	Mark 3:20–30
	Mark 7:1–2
	Mark 8:11–13a
	Mark 11:15–18
	Mark 12:13–34
	Mark 14:53–65
	Luke 5:27–39
	Luke 6:1–11
	Luke 11:14–23, 37–54
	Luke 13:31–35
	Luke 14:1–14
	Luke 20:1–8, 20–26, 27–40
	John 8:12–30
Peter	
Walking on the sea	Matthew 14:22–33
	Mark 6:45–56
	John 6:15–21
Declares his belief about Jesus	Matthew 16:13–20
	Mark 8:27–30
	Luke 9:18–21
Rebukes Jesus	Matthew 16:21–23
	Mark 8:31–33
Asks about the temple tax	Matthew 17:24–27
Asks about forgiveness	Matthew 18:21–35
Jesus predicts his denial	Matthew 26:31–35, 69–75
	Mark 14:27–31, 66–72
	Luke 22:31–34, 54–62
	John 13:33–38
	John 18:25–27
Peter, James, John (the transfiguration)	Matthew 17:1–13
	Mark 9:2–13
	Luke 9:28–36

Description (Who?)	Bible Reference
A group of children	Matthew 19:13–15 Mark 10:13–16 Luke 18:15–17
The Rich Young Man	Matthew 19:16–26 Mark 10:17–23 Luke 18:18–27
Mother of Zebedee's sons (James and John)	Matthew 20:20–23 Mark 10:35–40
Blind men outside of Jericho	Matthew 20:29–34 Mark 10:46–52 Luke 18:35–42
Moneychangers and salesmen in the temple	Matthew 21:12–17 Mark 11:15–19 Luke 19:45–48 John 2:13–22
The woman with perfume (home of Simon who suffered a skin disease)	Matthew 26:6–13 Mark 14:3–9 John 12:1–8
The trial in front of the Jewish Council	Matthew 26:57–68 Mark 14:53–65 Luke 22:63–71
Pilate	Matthew 27:11–26 Mark 15:1–15 Luke 23:1–25 John 18:28–40 John 19:4–15
Herod	Luke 23:5–12

Description (Who?)	Bible Reference
The soldiers	Matthew 27:27–30 Mark 15:16–19 John 19:1–3
Mary from Magdala and the other Mary (also Joanna, in Luke)	Matthew 28:1–10 Mark 16:1–8 Luke 24:1–12 John 20:1–18
The guards of Jesus' tomb	Matthew 28:11–15
The Canaanite (Matthew) or Greek (Mark) Woman	Matthew 15:22–28 Mark 7:24–30
The deaf and mute man from the Ten Cities	Mark 7:31–37
The blind man at Bethsaida	Mark 8:22–26
The shepherds near Bethlehem	Luke 2:8–20
Simeon	Luke 2:25–35
Anna	Luke 2:36–38
Teachers in the temple courts	Luke 2:41–50
A widow and her son	Luke 7:11–17
The sinful woman (cried at Jesus' feet)	Luke 7:36–50
The men who asked to follow Jesus (cost of following)	Luke 9:57–62

Description (Who?)	Bible Reference
An expert in the law (Good Samaritan parable)	Luke 10:25–37
Mary and Martha	Luke 10:38–42
Healing of Lazarus	John 11:1–44
Brother seeking his inheritance	Luke 12:13–21
A disabled woman	Luke 13:10–17
Zacchaeus	Luke 19:1–9
Criminals crucified with Jesus	Luke 23:39–43
Two men on the road to Emmaus	Luke 24:13–35
Jesus' mother and the servants	John 2:1–12
Nicodemus	John 3:1–21
Samaritan woman at the well	John 4:1–42
Man healed at the pool of Bethesda	John 5:1–15
Woman caught in adultery	John 8:1–11
Blind man at the Pool of Siloam	John 9:1–12, 35–41
Annas	John 18:12–14, 19–24
Thomas (after the resurrection)	John 20:24–29

The Holy Bible in Clear, Natural English

"GOD'S WORD® is an easy-to-understand Bible translation....It is a wonderful version."
~ REV. BILLY GRAHAM

GOD'S WORD Translation (GW) communicates the saving, life-changing Good News about Jesus in clear, natural English. Translated directly from the Hebrew, Aramaic, and Greek, GW is an exceptional Bible that consciously combines scholarly fidelity with natural English.

THE COMBINATION OF ACCURACY AND READABILITY MAKES **GW** IDEALLY SUITED FOR THE FOLLOWING:

- Devotional reading and in-depth study
- Preaching, teaching, and worship
- Memorization
- Discipleship

BakerBooks
a division of Baker Publishing Group

GOD'S WORD® TRANSLATION

Notes and commentary were provided by Jonathan Ziman, a Community Life Pastor at Wheaton Bible Church in Wheaton, Illinois, and leader of their Alpha evangelistic outreach program. He holds an MA from the University of Chicago and an MDiv from Trinity Evangelical Divinity School. Jonathan has worked as a freelance writer for the last ten years, contributing to devotional books, small group study guides, and study Bibles. Jonathan and his wife Kari have three young daughters and live in Wheaton.